I0441010

IN THE
YULE-LOG GLOW

Book II

Various Authors

THREE VOLUMES IN ONE.

*CHRISTMAS TALES FROM
'ROUND THE WORLD*

"Sic as folk tell ower at a winter ingle"
Scott

Editor: **Harrison S. Morris**

[ZHINGOORA BOOKS]

This edition is published by
Zhingoora Books.

The Cover is Designed by Pallav Sethiya.

CONTENTS OF BOOK II

A Droll Chapter by a Swiss Gossip.

"I here beheld an agreeable old

fellow, forgetting age, and showing

the way to be young at sixty-five."

Goldsmith.

CHRISTMAS WITH THE BARON.

I.

Once upon a time—fairy tales always begin with once upon a time—once upon a time there lived in a fine old castle on the Rhine a certain Baron von Schrochslofsleschshoffinger. You will not find it an easy name to pronounce; in fact, the baron never tried it himself but once, and then he was laid up for two days afterwards; so in future we will merely call him "the baron," for shortness, particularly as he was rather a dumpy man.

After having heard his name, you will not be surprised when I tell you that he was an exceedingly bad character. For a baron, he was considered enormously rich; a hundred and fifty pounds a year would not be thought much in this country; but still it will buy a good deal of sausage, which, with wine grown on the estate, formed the chief sustenance of the baron and his family.

Now, you will hardly believe that, notwithstanding he was the possessor of this princely revenue, the baron was not satisfied, but oppressed and ground down his unfortunate tenants to the very last penny he could possibly squeeze out of them. In all his exactions he was seconded and encouraged by his steward Klootz, an old rascal who took a malicious pleasure in his master's cruelty, and who chuckled and rubbed his hands with the greatest apparent enjoyment when any of the poor landholders could not pay their rent, or afforded him any opportunity for oppression.

Not content with making the poor tenants pay double value for the land they rented, the baron was in the habit of going round every now and then to their houses and ordering anything he took a fancy to, from a fat pig to a pretty daughter, to be sent up to the castle. The pretty daughter was made parlor-maid, but as she had nothing a year, and to find herself, it wasn't what would be considered by careful mothers an eligible situation. The fat pig became sausage, of course.

Things went on from bad to worse, till, at the time of our story, between the alternate squeezings of the baron and his steward, the poor tenants had very little left to squeeze out of them. The fat pigs and pretty daughters had nearly all found their way up to the castle, and there was little left to take.

The Daughter of the Baron

The only help the poor fellows had was the baron's only daughter, Lady Bertha, who always had a kind word, and frequently something more substantial, for them when her father was not in the way.

Now, I'm not going to describe Bertha, for the simple reason that if I did you would imagine that she was the fairy I'm going to tell you about, and she isn't. However, I don't mind giving you a few outlines.

In the first place, she was exceedingly tiny,—the nicest girls, the real lovable little pets, always are tiny,—and she had long silken black hair, and a dear, dimpled little face full of love and mischief. Now, then, fill up the outline with the details of the nicest and prettiest girl you know, and you will have a slight idea of her. On second thoughts, I don't believe you will, for your portrait wouldn't be half good enough; however, it will be near enough for you.

Well, the baron's daughter, being all your fancy painted her and a trifle more, was naturally much distressed at the goings-on of her unamiable parent, and tried her best to make amends for her father's harshness. She generally managed that a good many pounds of the sausage should find their way back to the owners of the original pig; and when the baron tried to squeeze the hand of the pretty parlor-maid, which he occasionally did after dinner, Bertha had only to say, in a tone of mild remonstrance, "Pa!" and he dropped the hand instantly and stared very hard the other way.

Bad as this disreputable old baron was, he had a respect for the goodness and purity of his child. Like the lion tamed by the charm of Una's innocence, the rough old rascal seemed to lose in her presence half his rudeness, and, though he used awful language to her sometimes (I dare say even Una's lion roared occasionally), he was more tractable with her than with any other living being. Her presence operated as a moral restraint upon him, which, possibly, was the reason that he never stayed down-stairs after dinner, but always retired to a favorite turret, which, I regret to say, he had got so in the way of doing every afternoon that I believe he would have felt unwell without it.

The hour of the baron's afternoon symposium was the time selected by Bertha for her errands of charity. Once he was fairly settled down to his second bottle, off went Bertha, with her maid beside her carrying a basket, to bestow a meal on some of the poor tenants, among whom she was always received with blessings.

At first these excursions had been undertaken principally from charitable motives, and Bertha thought herself plentifully repaid in the love and thanks of her grateful pensioners.

Of late, however, another cause had led her to take even stronger interest in her walks, and occasionally to come in with brighter eyes and a rosier cheek than the gratitude of the poor tenants had been wont to produce.

The fact is, some months before the time of our story, Bertha had noticed in her walks a young artist, who seemed to be fated to be invariably sketching points of interest in the road she had to take. There was one particular tree, exactly in the path which led from the castle-gate, which he had sketched from at least four points of view, and Bertha began to wonder what there could be so very particular about it.

At last, just as Carl von Sempach had begun to consider where on earth he could sketch the tree from next, and to ponder seriously upon the feasibility of climbing up into it and taking it from *that* point of view, a trifling accident occurred which gave him the opportunity of making Bertha's acquaintance,—which, I don't mind stating confidentially, was the very thing he had been waiting for.

It so chanced that, on one particular afternoon, the maid, either through awkwardness, or possibly through looking more at the handsome painter than the ground she was walking on, stumbled and fell.

Of course, the basket fell, too, and equally of course, Carl, as a gentleman, could not do less than offer his assistance in picking up the damsel and the dinner.

The acquaintance thus commenced was not suffered to drop; and handsome Carl and our good little Bertha were fairly over head and ears in love, and had begun to have serious thoughts of a cottage in a wood, *et cætera*, when their felicity was disturbed by their being accidentally met, in one of their walks, by the baron.

Of course the baron, being himself so thorough an aristocrat, had higher views for his daughter than marrying her to a "beggarly artist," and accordingly he stamped, and swore, and threatened Carl with summary punishment with all sorts of weapons, from heavy boots to blunderbusses, if ever he ventured near the premises again.

This was unpleasant; but I fear it did not *quite* put a stop to the young people's interviews, though it made them less frequent and more secret than before.

Now, I am quite aware this was not at all proper, and that no properly regulated young lady would ever have had meetings with a young man her papa didn't approve of.

But then it is just possible Bertha might not have been a properly regulated young lady. I only know she was a dear little pet, worth twenty model young ladies, and that she loved Carl very dearly.

And then consider what a dreadful old tyrant of a papa she had! My dear girl, it's not the slightest use your looking so provokingly correct; it's my deliberate belief that if you had been in her shoes (they'd have been at least three sizes too small for you, but that doesn't matter) you would have done precisely the same.

Such was the state of things on Christmas eve in the year—— Stay! fairy tales never have a year to them, so, on second thoughts, I wouldn't tell the date if I knew,—but I don't.

Such was the state of things, however, on the particular 24th of December to which our story refers—only, if anything, rather more so.

The baron had got up in the morning in an exceedingly bad temper; and those about him had felt its effects all through the day.

His two favorite wolf-hounds, Lutzow and Teufel, had received so many kicks from the baron's heavy boots that they hardly knew at which end their tails were; and even Klootz himself scarcely dared to approach his master.

In the middle of the day two of the principal tenants came to say that they were unprepared with their rent, and to beg for a little delay. The poor fellows represented that their families were starving, and entreated for mercy; but the baron was only too glad that he had at last found so fair an excuse for venting his ill-humor.

He loaded the unhappy defaulters with every abusive epithet he could devise (and being called names in German is no joke, I can tell you); and, lastly, he swore by everything he could think of that, if their rent was not paid on the morrow, themselves and their families should be turned out of doors to sleep on the snow, which was then many inches deep on the ground. They still continued to beg for mercy, till the baron became so exasperated that he determined to put them out of the castle himself. He pursued them for that purpose as far as the outer door, when fresh fuel was added to his anger.

Carl, who, as I have hinted, still managed, notwithstanding the paternal prohibition, to see Bertha occasionally, and had come to wish her a merry Christmas, chanced at this identical moment to be saying good-bye at the door, above which, in accordance with immemorial usage, a huge bush of mistletoe was suspended. What they were doing under it at the moment of the baron's appearance, I never knew exactly; but his wrath was tremendous!

I regret to say that his language was unparliamentary in the extreme. He swore until he was mauve in the face; and if he had not providentially been seized with a fit of coughing, and sat down in the coal-scuttle,—mistaking it for a three-legged stool,—it is impossible to say to what lengths his feelings might have carried him.

Carl and Bertha picked him up, rather black behind, but otherwise not much the worse for his accident.

In fact, the diversion of his thoughts seemed to have done him good; for, having sworn a little more, and Carl having left the castle, he appeared rather better.

II.

After enduring so many and various emotions, it is hardly to be wondered at that the baron required some consolation; so, after having changed his trousers, he took himself off to his favorite turret to allay, by copious potations, the irritations of his mind.

Bottle after bottle was emptied, and pipe after pipe was filled and smoked. The fine old Burgundy was gradually getting into the baron's head; and, altogether, he was beginning to feel more comfortable.

The shades of the winter afternoon had deepened into the evening twilight, made dimmer still by the aromatic clouds that came, with dignified deliberation, from the baron's lips, and curled and floated up to the carved ceiling of the turret, where they spread themselves into a dim canopy, which every successive cloud brought lower and lower.

The fire, which had been piled up mountain-high earlier in the afternoon, and had flamed and roared to its heart's content ever since, had now got to that state—the perfection of a fire to a lazy man—when it requires no poking or attention of any kind, but just burns itself hollow, and then tumbles in, and blazes jovially for a little time, and then settles down to a genial glow, and gets hollow, and tumbles in again.

The baron's fire was just in this delightful *da capo* condition, most favorable of all to the enjoyment of the *dolce far niente.*

For a little while it would glow and kindle quietly, making strange faces to itself, and building fantastic castles in the depths of its red recesses, and then the castles would come down with a crash, and the faces disappear, and a bright flame spring up and lick lovingly the sides of the old chimney; and the carved heads of improbable men and impossible women, hewn so deftly round the panels of the old oak wardrobe opposite, in which the baron's choicest vintages were deposited, were lit up by the flickering light, and seemed to nod and wink at the fire in return, with the familiarity of old acquaintances.

Some such fancy as this was disporting itself in the baron's brain; and he was gazing at the old oak carving accordingly, and emitting huge volumes of smoke with reflective slowness, when a clatter among the bottles on the table caused him to turn his head to ascertain the cause.

The baron was by no means a nervous man; however, the sight that met his eyes when he turned round did take away his presence of mind a little; and he was obliged to take four distinct puffs before he had sufficiently regained his equilibrium to inquire, "Who the—Pickwick—are you?" (The baron said "Dickens," but, as that is a naughty word, we will substitute "Pickwick," which is equally expressive, and not so wrong.) Let me see; where was I? Oh, yes! "Who the Pickwick are you?"

Now, before I allow the baron's visitor to answer the question, perhaps I had better give a slight description of his personal appearance.

If this was not a true story, I should have liked to have made him a model of manly beauty; but a regard for veracity compels me to confess that he was not what would be generally considered handsome; that is, not in figure, for his face was by no means unpleasing.

His body was, in size and shape, not very unlike a huge plum-pudding, and was clothed in a bright-green, tightly-fitting doublet, with red holly-berries for buttons.

His limbs were long and slender in proportion to his stature, which was not more than three feet or so.

His head was encircled by a crown of holly and mistletoe.

The round red berries sparkled amid his hair which was silver-white, and shone out in cheerful harmony with his rosy, jovial face. And that face! it would have done one good to look at it.

In spite of the silver hair, and an occasional wrinkle beneath the merry, laughing eyes, it seemed brimming over with perpetual youth. The mouth, well garnished with teeth, white and sound, which seemed as if they could do ample justice to holiday cheer, was ever open with a beaming, genial smile, expanding now and then into hearty laughter. Fun and good-fellowship were in every feature.

The owner of the face was, at the moment when the baron first perceived him, comfortably seated upon the top of the large tobacco-jar on the table, nursing his left leg.

The baron's somewhat abrupt inquiry did not appear to irritate him; on the contrary, he seemed rather amused than otherwise.

"You don't ask prettily, old gentleman," he replied; "but I don't mind telling you, for all that. I'm King Christmas."

"Eh?" said the baron.

"Ah!" said the goblin. Of course, you have guessed he was a goblin?

"And pray what's your business here?" said the baron.

"Don't be crusty with a fellow," replied the goblin. "I merely looked in to wish you the compliments of the season. Talking of crust, by the way, what sort of a tap is it you're drinking?" So saying, he took up a flask of the baron's very best and poured out about half a glass. Having held the glass first on one side and then on the other, winked at it twice, sniffed it, and gone through the remainder of the pantomime in which connoisseurs indulge, he drank it with great deliberation, and smacked his lips scientifically. "Hum! Johannisberg! and not so *very* bad—for you. But I tell you what it is, baron, you'll have to bring out better stuff than this when I put my legs on your mahogany."

"Well, you are a cool fish," said the baron. "However, you're rather a joke, so, now you're here, we may as well enjoy ourselves. Smoke?"

"Not anything you're likely to offer me!"

"Confound your impudence!" roared the baron, with a horribly complicated oath. "That tobacco is as good as any in all Rhineland."

"That's a nasty cough you've got, baron. Don't excite yourself, my dear boy; I dare say you speak according to your lights. I don't mean Vesuvians, you know, but your opportunities for knowing anything about it. Try a weed out of my case, and I expect you'll alter your opinion."

The baron took the proffered case and selected a cigar. Not a word was spoken till it was half consumed, when the baron took it, for the first time, from his lips, and said, gently, with the air of a man communicating an important discovery in the strictest confidence, "Das ist gut!"

"Thought you'd say so," said the visitor. "And now, as you like the cigar, I should like you to try a thimbleful of what I call wine. I must warn you, though, that it is rather potent, and may produce effects you are not accustomed to."

"Bother that, if it is as good as the weed," said the baron; "I haven't taken my usual quantity by four bottles yet."

"Well, don't say I didn't warn you, that's all. I don't think you'll find it unpleasant, though it is rather strong when you're not accustomed to it." So saying, the goblin produced from some mysterious pocket a black, big-bellied bottle, crusted, apparently, with the dust of ages.

It did strike the baron as peculiar, that the bottle, when once produced, appeared nearly as big round as the goblin himself; but he was not the sort of man to stick at trifles, and he pushed forward his glass to be filled just as composedly as if the potion had been shipped and paid duty, in the most commonplace way.

The glass was filled and emptied, but the baron uttered not his opinion. Not in words, at least, but he pushed forward his glass to be filled again in a manner that sufficiently bespoke his approval.

"Aha! you smile!" said the goblin. And it was a positive fact; the baron was smiling; a thing he had not been known to do in the memory of the oldest inhabitant. "That's the stuff to make your hair curl, isn't it?"

"I believe you, my b-o-o-oy!" The baron brought out this earnest expression of implicit confidence with true unction. "It warms one *here*!"

Knowing the character of the man, one would have expected him to put his hand upon his stomach. But he didn't; he laid it upon his *heart*.

"The spell begins to operate, I see," said the goblin. "Have another glass?"

The baron had another glass, and another after that.

The smile on his face expanded into an expression of such geniality that the whole character of his countenance was changed, and his own mother wouldn't have known him. I doubt myself—inasmuch as she died when he was exactly a year and three months old—whether she would have recognized him under any circumstances; but I merely wish to express that he was changed almost beyond recognition.

"Upon my word," said the baron, at length, "I feel so light I almost think I could dance a hornpipe. I used to, once, I know. Shall I try?"

"Well, if you ask my advice," replied the goblin, "I should say, decidedly, don't. 'Barkis is willing,' I dare say, but trousers are weak, and you might split 'em."

"Hang it all," said the baron, "so I might. I didn't think of that. But still I feel as if I must do something juvenile!"

"Ah! that's the effect of your change of nature," said the goblin. "Never mind, I'll give you plenty to do presently."

"Change of nature! What do you mean, you old conundrum?" said the baron.

"You're another," said the goblin. "But never mind. What I mean is just this. What you are now feeling is the natural consequence of my magic wine, which has changed you into a fairy. That's what's the matter, sir."

"A fairy! me!" exclaimed the baron. "Get out. I'm too fat."

"Fat! Oh! that's nothing. We shall put you in regular training, and you'll soon be slim enough to creep into a lady's stocking. Not that you'll be called upon to do anything of the sort; but I'm merely giving you an idea of your future figure."

"No, no," said the baron; "me thin! that's too ridiculous. Why, that's worse than being a fairy. You don't mean it, though, do you? I do feel rather peculiar."

"I do, indeed," said the visitor. "You don't dislike it, do you?"

"Well, no, I can't say I do, entirely. It's queer, though, I feel so uncommon friendly. I feel as if I should like to shake hands or pat somebody on the back."

"Ah!" said the goblin, "I know how it is. Rum feeling, when you're not accustomed to it. But come; finish that glass, for we must be off. We've got a precious deal to do before morning, I can tell you. Are you ready?"

"All right," said the baron. "I'm just in the humor to make a night of it."

"Come along, then," said the goblin.

They proceeded for a short time in silence along the corridors of the old castle. They carried no candle, but the baron noticed that everything seemed perfectly light wherever they stood, but relapsed into darkness as soon as they had passed by. The goblin spoke first.

"I say, baron, you've been an uncommon old brute in your time, now, haven't you?"

"H'm," said the baron, reflectively; "I don't know. Well, yes, I rather think I have."

"How jolly miserable you've been making those two young people, you old sinner! You know who I mean."

"Eh, what? You know that, too?" said the baron.

"Know it; of course I do. Why, bless your heart, I know everything, my dear boy. But you *have* made yourself an old tyrant in that quarter, considerably. Ar'n't you blushing, you hard-hearted old monster?"

"Don't know, I'm sure," said the baron, scratching his nose, as if that was where he expected to feel it. "I believe I have treated them badly, though, now I come to think of it."

At this moment they reached the door of Bertha's chamber The door opened of itself at their approach.

"Come along," said the goblin; "you won't wake her. Now, old flinty-heart, look there."

The sight that met the baron's view was one that few fathers could have beheld without affectionate emotion. Under ordinary circumstances, however, the baron would not have felt at all sentimental on the subject, but to-night something made him view things in quite a different light.

I shouldn't like to make affidavit of the fact, but it's my positive impression that he sighed.

Now, my dear reader, don't imagine I'm going to indulge your impertinent curiosity with an elaborate description of the sacred details of a lady's sleeping apartment. *You're* not a fairy, you know, and I don't see that it can possibly matter to you whether fair Bertha's dainty little bottines were tidily placed on a chair by her bedside, or thrown carelessly, as they had been taken off, upon the hearth-rug, where her favorite spaniel reposed, warming his nose in his sleep before the last smouldering embers of the decaying fire; or whether her crinoline—but if she did wear a crinoline, what can that possibly matter to you?

All I shall tell you is, that everything looked snug and comfortable; but, somehow, any place got that look when Bertha was in it.

And now a word about the jewel in the casket—pet Bertha herself. Really, I'm at a loss to describe her. How do you look when you're asleep?—Well, it wasn't like *that*; not a bit! Fancy a sweet girl's face, the cheek faintly flushed with a soft, warm tint, like the blush in the heart of the opening rose, and made brighter by the contrast of the snowy pillow on which it rested; dark silken hair, curling and clustering lovingly over the tiniest of tiny ears, and the softest, whitest neck that ever mortal maiden was blessed with; long silken eyelashes, fringing lids only less beautiful than the dear earnest eyes they cover. Fancy all this, and fancy, too, if you can, the expression of perfect goodness and purity that lit up the sweet features of the slumbering maiden with a beauty almost angelic, and you will see what the baron saw that night. Not quite all, however, for the baron's vision paused not at the bedside before him, but had passed on from the face of the sleeping maiden to another face as lovely, that of the young wife, Bertha's mother, who had, years before, taken her angel beauty to the angels.

The goblin spoke to the baron's thought. "Wonderfully like her, is she not, baron?" The baron slowly inclined his head.

"You made her very happy, didn't you?"

The tone in which the goblin spoke was harsh and mocking.

"A faithful husband, tender and true! She must have been a happy wife, eh, baron?"

The baron's head had sunk upon his bosom. Old recollections were thronging into his awakened memory. Solemn vows to love and cherish somewhat strangely kept. Memories of bitter words and savage oaths showered at a quiet and uncomplaining figure, without one word in reply. And, last, the memory of a fit of drunken passion, and a hasty blow struck with a heavy hand. And then of three months of fading away; and last, of her last prayer—for her baby and him.

"A good husband makes a good father, baron. No wonder you are somewhat chary of rashly intrusting to a suitor the happiness of a sweet flower like this. Poor child! it is hard, though, that she must think no more of him she loves so dearly. See! she is weeping even in her dreams. But you have good reasons, no doubt. Young Carl is wild, perhaps, or drinks, or gambles, eh? What! none of these? Perhaps he is wayward and uncertain; and you fear that the honeyed words of courtship might turn to bitter sayings in matrimony. They do, sometimes, eh, baron? By all means guard her from such a fate as that. Poor, tender flower! Or who knows, worse than that, baron! Hard words break no bones, they say, but angry men are quick, and a blow is soon struck, eh?"

The goblin had drawn nearer and nearer, and laid his hand upon the baron's arm, and the last words were literally hissed into his ears.

The baron's frame swayed to and fro under the violence of his emotion. At last, with a cry of agony, he dashed his hands upon his forehead. The veins were swollen up like thick cords, and his voice was almost inarticulate in its unnatural hoarseness.

"Tortures! release me! Let me go, let me go and do something to forget the past, or I shall go mad and die!"

He rushed out of the room and paced wildly down the corridor, the goblin following him. At last, as they came near the outer door of the castle, which opened of itself as they reached it, the spirit spoke:

"This way, baron, this way. I told you there was work for us to do before morning, you know."

"Work!" exclaimed the baron, absently, passing his fingers through his tangled hair; "oh! yes, work! the harder the better; anything to make me forget."

The two stepped out into the court-yard, and the baron shivered, though, as it seemed, unconsciously, at the breath of the frosty midnight air. The snow lay deep on the ground, and the baron's heavy boots sank into it with a crisp, crushing sound at every tread.

He was bareheaded, but seemed unconscious of the fact, and tramped on, as if utterly indifferent to anything but his own thoughts. At last, as a blast of the night wind, keener than ordinary, swept over him, he seemed for the first time to feel the chill. His teeth chattered, and he muttered, "Cold, very cold."

"Ay, baron," said the goblin, "it is cold even to us, who are healthy and strong, and warmed with wine. Colder still, though, to those who are hungry and half-naked, and have to sleep on the snow."

"Sleep? snow?" said the baron. "Who sleeps on the snow? Why, I wouldn't let my dogs be out on such a night as this."

"Your dogs, no!" said the goblin; "I spoke of meaner animals—your wretched tenants. Did you not order, yesterday, that Wilhelm and Friedrich, if they did not pay their rent to-morrow, should be turned out to sleep on the snow? A snug bed for the little ones, and a nice white coverlet, eh? Ha! ha! twenty florins or so is no great matter, is it? I'm afraid their chance is small; nevertheless, come and see."

The baron hung his head. A few minutes brought him to the first of the poor dwellings, which they entered noiselessly. The fireless grate, the carpetless floor, the broken window-panes, all gave sufficient testimony to the want and misery of the occupants. In one corner lay sleeping a man, a woman, and three children, and nestling to each other for the warmth which their ragged coverlet could afford. In the man, the baron recognized his tenant Wilhelm, one of those who had been with him to beg for indulgence on the previous day.

The keen features, and bones almost starting through the pallid skin, showed how heavily the hand of hunger had been laid upon all.

The cold night wind moaned and whistled through the many flaws in the ill-glazed, ill-thatched tenement, and rustled over the sleepers, who shivered even in their sleep.

"Ha, baron!" said the goblin, "death is breathing in their faces even now, you see; it is hardly worth while to lay them to sleep in the snow, is it? They would sleep a little sounder, that's all."

The baron shuddered, and then, hastily pulling the warm coat from his own shoulders, he spread it over the sleepers.

"Oho!" said the goblin; "bravely done, baron! By all means keep them warm to-night; they enjoy the snow more to-morrow, you know."

Strange to say, the baron, instead of feeling chilled when he had removed his coat, felt a strange glow of warmth spread from the region of the heart over his entire frame. The goblin's continual allusions to his former intention, which he had by this time totally relinquished, hurt him, and he said, rather pathetically,—

"Don't talk of that again, good goblin. I'd rather sleep on the snow myself."

"Eh! what?" said the goblin; "you don't mean to say you're sorry? Then what do you say to making these poor people comfortable?"

"With all my heart," said the baron, "if we had only anything to do it with."

"You leave that to me," said the goblin. "Your brother fairies are not far off, you may be sure."

As he spoke he clapped his hands thrice, and before the third clap had died away the poor cottage was swarming with tiny figures, whom the baron rightly conjectured to be the fairies themselves.

Now, you may not be aware (the baron was not, until that night) that there are among the fairies trades and professions, just as with ordinary mortals.

However, there they were, each with the accompaniments of his or her particular business, and to it they went manfully. A fairy glazier put in new panes to the shattered windows, fairy carpenters replaced the doors upon their hinges, and fairy painters, with inconceivable celerity, made cupboards and closets as fresh as paint could make them; one fairy housemaid laid and lit a roaring fire, while another dusted and rubbed chairs and tables to a miraculous degree of brightness; a fairy butler uncorked bottles of fairy wine, and a fairy cook laid out a repast of most tempting appearance.

The baron, hearing a tapping above him, cast his eyes upward, and beheld a fairy slater rapidly repairing a hole in the roof; and when he bent them down again they fell on a fairy doctor mixing a cordial for the sleepers. Nay, there was even a fairy parson, who, not having any present employment, contented himself with rubbing his hands and looking pleasant, probably waiting till somebody might want to be christened or married.

Every trade, every profession or occupation appeared, without exception, to be represented; nay, we beg pardon, with one exception only, for the baron used to say, when afterwards relating his experiences to bachelor friends,—

"You may believe me or not, sir, there was every mortal business under the sun, *but deil a bit of a lawyer.*"

The baron could not long remain inactive. He was rapidly seized with a violent desire to do something to help, which manifested itself in insane attempts to assist everybody at once. At last, after having taken all the skin off his knuckles in attempting to hammer in nails in aid of the carpenter, and then nearly tumbling over a fairy housemaid, whose broom he was offering to carry, he gave it up as a bad job, and stood aside with his friend the goblin.

He was just about to inquire how it was that the poor occupants of the house were not awakened by so much din, when a fairy Sam Slick, who had been examining the cottager's old clock with a view to a thorough repair, touched some spring within it, and it made the usual purr preparatory to striking. When, lo! and behold, at the very first stroke, cottage, goblin, fairies, and all disappeared into utter darkness, and the baron found himself in his turret-chamber, rubbing his toe, which he had just hit with considerable force against the fender. As he was only in his slippers, the concussion was unpleasant, and the baron rubbed his toe for a good while.

After he had finished with his toe he rubbed his nose, and, finally, with a countenance of deep reflection, scratched the bump of something or other at the top of his head.

The old clock on the stairs was striking three, and the fire had gone out.

The baron reflected for a short time longer, and finally decided that he had better go to bed, which he did accordingly.

III.

The morning dawned upon the very ideal, as far as weather was concerned, of a Christmas-day. A bright winter sun shone out just vividly enough to make everything look genial and pleasant, and yet not with sufficient warmth to mar the pure, unbroken surface of the crisp, white snow, which lay like a never-ending white lawn upon the ground, and glittered in myriad silver flakes upon the leaves of the sturdy evergreens.

I am afraid the baron had not had a very good night; at any rate, I know that he was wide-awake at an hour long before his usual time of rising.

He lay first on one side, and then on the other, and then, by way of variety, turned on his back, with his magenta nose pointing perpendicularly towards the ceiling; but it was all of no use. Do what he would, he couldn't get to sleep, and at last, not long after daybreak, he tumbled out of bed and proceeded to dress.

Even after he was out of bed his fidgetiness continued. It did not strike him, until after he had got one boot on, that it would be a more natural proceeding to put his stockings on first; after which he caught himself in the act of trying to put his trousers on over his head.

In a word, the baron's mind was evidently preoccupied; his whole air was that of a man who felt a strong impulse to do something or other, but could not quite make up his mind to it.

At last, however, the good impulse conquered, and this wicked old baron, in the stillness of the calm, bright Christmas morning, went down upon his knees and prayed.

Stiff were his knees and slow his tongue, for neither had done such work for many a long day past; but I have read in the Book of the joy of angels over a repenting sinner.

There needs not much eloquence to pray the publican's prayer, and who shall say but there was gladness in heaven that Christmas morning?

The baron's appearance down-stairs at such an early hour occasioned quite a commotion. Nor were the domestics reassured when the baron ordered a bullock to be killed and jointed instantly, and all the available provisions in the larder, including sausage, to be packed up in baskets, with a good store of his own peculiar wine.

One ancient retainer was heard to declare, with much pathos, that he feared master had gone insane.

However, insane or not, they knew the baron must be obeyed, and in an exceedingly short space of time he sallied forth, accompanied by three servants carrying the baskets, and wondering what in the name of fortune their master would do next.

He stopped at the cottage of Wilhelm, which he had visited with the goblin on the previous night. The labors of the fairies did not seem to have produced much lasting benefit, for the appearance of everything around was as wretched as could be.

The poor family thought that the baron had come himself to turn them out of house and home; and the children huddled up timidly to their mother for protection, while the father attempted some words of entreaty for mercy.

The pale, pinched features of the group, and their looks of dread and wretchedness, were too much for the baron.

"Eh! what! what do you mean, confound you? Turn you out? Of course not: I've brought you some breakfast. Here! Fritz—Carl; where are the knaves? Now, then, unpack, and don't be a week about it. Can't you see the people are hungry, ye villains? Here, lend me the corkscrew."

This last being a tool the baron was tolerably accustomed to, he had better success than with those of the fairy carpenters; and it was not long before the poor tenants were seated before a roaring fire, and doing justice, with the appetite of starvation, to a substantial breakfast.

The baron felt a queer sensation in his throat at the sight of the poor people's enjoyment, and had passed the back of his hand twice across his eyes when he thought no one was looking; but his emotion fairly rose to boiling when the poor father, Wilhelm, with tears in his eyes, and about a quarter of a pound of beef in his mouth, sprang up from the table and flung himself at the baron's knees, invoking blessings on him for his goodness.

"Get up, you audacious scoundrel!" roared the baron. "What the deuce do you mean by such conduct, eh? confound you!"

At this moment the door opened, and in walked Mynheer Klootz, who had heard nothing of the baron's change of intentions, and who, seeing Wilhelm at the baron's feet, and hearing the latter speaking, as he thought, in an angry tone, at once jumped to the conclusion that Wilhelm was entreating for longer indulgence. He rushed at the unfortunate man and collared him. "Not if we know it," exclaimed he; "you'll have the wolves for bedfellows to-night, I reckon. Come along, my fine fellow." As he spoke he turned his back towards the baron, with the intention of dragging his victim to the door.

The baron's little gray eyes twinkled, and his whole frame quivered with suppressed emotion, which, after the lapse of a moment, vented itself in a kick, and such a kick! Not one of your *varsovianna* flourishes, but a kick that employed every muscle from hip to toe, and drove the worthy steward up against the door like a ball from a catapult.

Misfortunes never come singly, and so Mynheer Klootz found with regard to the kick, for it was followed, without loss of time, by several dozen others, as like it as possible, from the baron's heavy boots.

Wounded lions proverbially come badly off, and Fritz and Carl, who had suffered from many an act of petty tyranny on the part of the steward, thought they could not do better than follow their master's example, which they did to such good purpose, that when the unfortunate Klootz did escape from the cottage at last, I don't believe he could have had any os sacrum left.

After having executed this little act of poetical justice, the baron and his servants visited the other cottages, in all of which they were received with dread and dismissed with blessings.

Having completed his tour of charity, the baron returned home to breakfast, feeling more really contented than he had done for many a long year. He found Bertha, who had not risen when he started, in a considerable state of anxiety as to what he could possibly have been doing. In answer to her inquiries, he told her, with a roughness he was far from feeling, to "mind her own affairs."

The gentle eyes filled with tears at the harshness of the reply; perceiving which, the baron was beyond measure distressed, and chucked her under the chin in what was meant to be a very conciliatory manner.

"Eh! what, my pretty, tears? No, surely. Bertha must forgive her old father. I didn't mean it, you know, my pet; and yet, on second thoughts, yes, I did, too." Bertha's face was overcast again. "My little girl thinks she has no business anywhere, eh! Is that it? Well, then, my pet, suppose you make it your business to write a note to young Carl von Sempach, and say I'm afraid I was rather rude to him yesterday, but if he'll overlook it, and come take a snug family dinner and a slice of the pudding with us to-day——"

"Why, pa, you don't mean—yes, I do really believe you do——"

The baron's eyes were winking nineteen to the dozen.

"Why, you dear, dear, dear old pa!" and at the imminent risk of upsetting the breakfast table, Bertha rushed at the baron, and flinging two soft white arms about his neck, kissed him—oh! how she *did* kiss him! I shouldn't have thought, myself, she could possibly have had any left for Carl; but I dare say Bertha attended to his interests in that respect somehow.

IV.

Well, Carl came to dinner, and the baron was, not very many years after, promoted to the dignity of a grandpapa, and a very jolly old grandpapa he made.

Is that all you wanted to know? About Klootz? Well, Klootz got over the kicking, but he was dismissed from the baron's service; and on examination of his accounts it was discovered that he had been in the habit of robbing the baron of nearly a third of his yearly income, which he had to refund; and with the money he was thus compelled to disgorge, the baron built new cottages for his tenants, and new-stocked their farms. Nor was he poorer in the end, for his tenants worked with the energy of gratitude, and he was soon many times richer than when the goblin visited him on that Christmas eve.

And was the goblin ever explained? Certainly not. How dare you have the impertinence to suppose such a thing?

An empty bottle, covered with cobwebs, was found the next morning in the turret-chamber, which the baron at first imagined must be the bottle from which the goblin produced his magic wine; but as it was found, on examination, to be labelled "Old Jamaica Rum," of course that could not have had anything to do with it. However it was, the baron never thoroughly enjoyed any other wine after it, and as he did not thenceforth get intoxicated, on an average, more than two nights a week, or swear more than eight oaths a day, I think King Christmas may be considered to have thoroughly reformed him.

And he always maintained, to the day of his death, that he was changed into a fairy, and became exceedingly angry if contradicted.

Who doesn't believe in fairies after this? I only hope King Christmas may make a few more good fairies this year, to brighten the homes of the poor with the light of Christmas charity.

Truly, we need not look far for alms-men. Cold and hunger, disease and death, are around us at all times; but at no time do they press more heavily on the poor than at this jovial Christmas season.

Shall we shut out, in our mirth and jollity, the cry of the hungry poor? or shall we not rather remember, in the midst of our happy family circles, round our well-filled tables and before our blazing fires, that our brothers are starving out in the cold, and that the Christmas song of the angels was "Good-will to men"?

The Spaniard's Episode.

"He was a pleasant-looking fellow,

with huge black whiskers

and a roguish eye. He touched

the guitar with masterly skill,

and sang little amorous ditties

with an expressive leer."

Irving.

A CHRISTMAS MIRACLE.

You have never heard of Alcala? Well, it is a little village nestling between the Spanish hills, a league from great Madrid. There is a ring of stone houses, each with its white-walled patio and grated windows; each with its balcony, whence now and then a laughing face looks down upon the traveller. There is an ancient inn by the roadside, a time-worn church, and above, on the hill-top, against the still blue sky, the castle, dusky with age, but still keeping a feudal dignity, though half its yellow walls have crumbled away.

This is the Alcala into which I jogged one winter evening in search of rest and entertainment after a long day's journey on mule-back.

The inn was in a doze when my footsteps broke the silence of its stone court-yard; but presently a woman came through an inner door to answer my summons, and I was speedily cast under the quiet spell of the place by finding myself behind a screen of leaves, with a straw-covered bottle at my elbow and a cold fowl within comfortable reach.

The bower where I sat was unlighted save by the waning sun, and I could see but little of its long vista, without neglecting a very imperious appetite. The lattice was covered, I thought, with vine-leaves, and I felt sure, too, that some orange boughs, reaching across the patio wall, mingled with the foliage above my head. But all I was certain of was the relish of the fowl and the delicious refreshment of the cool wine. Having finished these, I lay back in my chair, luxuriating in the sense of healthy fatigue, and going over again, in fancy, the rolling roads of my journey.

I believe I, also, fell into the prevailing slumber of the place, lulled by the soft atmosphere and gentle wine, and might have slept there till morning had a furious sneeze not awakened me with a start. I looked confusedly about in the dusk, but could see nothing save, at last, the tip of a lighted cigarette in the remote depths of the bower. I called out,—

"Who's there?" and was answered, courteously, by a deep, gruff voice in Spanish,—

"It is I, señor, Jose Rosado."

"Are you a guest of 'La Fonda'?" said I, for I had learned that this was the name of the inn, and was a little doubtful whether I had fallen into the hands of friend or foe.

"Ha! ha! ha!" with a long explosion of guttural sounds, was my only answer. Then, after a brightening of the cigarette-fire, to denote that the smoker was puffing it into life, he said,—

"I, señor, am the host."

At this I drew my chair closer, and found, in the thin reflection of the cigarette, a round, bronzed face beaming with smiles and picturing easy good health.

It was winter in Spain, but the scent of flowers was abroad, and the soft, far-off stars twinkled through the moving leaves. What wonder, then, that we fell into talk,—I, the inquiring traveller, he, the arch-gossip of Alcala,—and talked till the moon rose high into the night?

"And who lives in the castle on the hill?" I asked, after hearing the private history of half the town.

"Ah," said mine host, as if preparing to swallow a savory morsel, "there's a bit of gossip; there's a story, indeed!" He puffed away for a minute in mute satisfaction, and then began.

"That is a noble family, the Aranjuez. None can remember in Alcala when there was not a noble Aranjuez living in its castle, and they have led our people bravely in all the wars of Spain. I remember as a boy——"

But, having become acquainted with mine host's loquacity, I broke in with a question more to the point,—

"Who, Señor Jose, lives in the castle now?"

He would have answered without a suspicion of my ruse, had not a bell just then rung solemnly forth, awakening the still night, and arousing Jose Rosado from his comfortable bench, promptly to his feet.

"Come," he said; "that is for the Christmas Mass. I will tell you as we go."

The little inn was lively enough as we emerged from the bower and crossed the court-yard towards the road. The woman who had prepared my supper came forth arrayed in a capulet of white and scarlet, and two younger girls who accompanied her wore veils and long, black robes which fell about their forms like Oriental garments. Two or three men, attendants and hostlers of the place, were also about to start, trigged out in queer little capes and high-crowned hats. All this fine apparel, mine host informed me, was peculiar to Christmas, and I soon found the highway full of peasants in similar garb.

As we got off, Jose Rosado resumed his story, which was brief enough to beguile us just to the church-door.

"You ask me, señor, who lives in the castle now? The Donna Isabella is alone there, now, the only survivor of the noble race, except—except señor," (he laid a peculiar emphasis on the word,) "except a wilful son, whom she has disowned and driven from her house. He is a handsome lad, and married, here in Alcala, the beauty of the town, in spite of his mother's wounded pride. It was a love-match of stolen wooing and secret wedding,—but, ha! ha! we saw it all, knew it all, before even they did themselves. Many an evening have I met them on these roads, billing and cooing like the doves on La Fonda's eaves. They were made by nature for each other, though, and even the rage of the proud Donna Isabella could never part them."

"And do they still live in the town?" I asked.

"Oh, yes," said Jose; "over there in the white house where the olive trees are, at the bottom of the long hill."

I looked in the direction whither he pointed, but I could see little in the dim moonlight save a white wall amid dense shadows.

"And is Donna Isabella a very old lady?" I asked, because very old ladies are often charged with peculiar severity to very young ones.

"No, no, no," said Jose Rosado, with a quick turn of the head to each no. "She's a widow lady of middle age; very proud and very handsome. You shall see her presently, for she has consented to take part in the Christmas play at the church."

As I had come a long journey to see this same Christmas play, my expectation was doubly aroused as we approached the old edifice, whose open belfry and rows of cloisters stood before us at the top of the hill we were ascending.

As we entered, the bells stopped ringing, for it was precisely midnight, and the priest at the altar began to say the Christmas Masses. When he had reached the Gospel, he was interrupted by the appearance of a matron, dressed all in white, who stood at the end of the nave. She was clad like the Madonna, and was accompanied by Joseph, who wore the garb of a mountaineer, with a hatchet in his hand. An officious little officer with a halberd opened the way through the crowd before these personages, and they came solemnly up the aisle towards the chancel, which had been arrayed to represent Bethlehem, the Madonna reciting, as she moved forward, a plaintive song about her homelessness. Joseph replied cheeringly, and led her under a roof of leaves in the sanctuary, formed in the manner of a stable, in which we could see the manger against the wall. Here she took rest from her journey, while a little crib, wherein lay the Bambino—or waxen image of the Babe—all adorned with ribbons and laces, was brought from the sacristy and placed in the straw at her feet.

As the Madonna passed us, Jose Rosado nudged me, and whispered audibly enough to make the crowd about us turn and stare,—

"Hist! here's the Donna Isabella, señor! She looks like a saint to-night!"

I watched her closely as she went by me, and marked, under the meek expression assumed by the Virgin, a more characteristic one of severe resolution. She was, however, a queenly woman, in the ripest stage of maturity, but she bore herself, in the part she had taken, with a matronly grace something too conscious for the lowly Mary.

As she seated herself on the heap of straw, a little boy in a surplice, representing an angel, with wings of crimped lawn at his shoulders, was raised in a chair, by a cord and pulley, to the very top of the sanctuary arch, where he sang a carol to the shepherds,—

"Shepherds, hasten allWith flying feet from your retreat;On rustic pipes now playYour sweetest, sweetest lay;

for"—so ran the song—"Mary and the King of Heaven are in yonder cave."

At this, an orchestra, concealed behind the high altar, set up a tooting from bagpipes, and flute, and violin, which served as a prelude to the appearance of the shepherds, who were concealed in the gallery.

Up they got, with long cloaks and crooked staffs, murmuring their surprise and incredulity at what the angel had said; some pretending to grumble at being awakened from sleep, others anxious to prove the truth of the strange tidings.

Then the angel sang a more appealing ditty still, whereat they were all about ready to advance, when one of their number, of a sceptical turn, urged them to avoid such fanciful matters and give heed to their sheep, who would otherwise become the prey of the wolf.

Hereupon, an old shepherd appeared, who gave three loud knocks with his crook, and denounced those who should disobey the heavenly messenger. The practical man was thus silenced, and they expressed their willingness to go to the manger,—and at the same moment an angel appeared to guide them thither.

They descended from the gallery to the outer porch of the church and knocked loudly at the door, saying, as if to the innkeeper at Bethlehem:

"Pray, good master of the inn, Open the door and let us in."

But Joseph became alarmed at the approach of such a number of rustics, and inquired who they were. They held a songful colloquy with him; but he continued to refuse them admittance, until an angel again intervened, this time in the form of a tall acolyte from the sanctuary, accompanied by two little angelic choristers. He reassured Joseph, and invited the shepherds to enter and worship the Babe. They came up the aisle flourishing their be-ribboned crooks and singing in praise of the Child, but they were sorely vexed, when they saw the stable, that so humble a place had been found for His shelter. Joseph explained, in several couplets, that no other house would receive them, and the shepherds replied in several others, mingling sympathy and good advice, intended not for Joseph, but for the throng, who listened in religious awe.

After paying due homage to the child and Mary, the shepherds exchanged some more verses with Joseph, and then retired to the other end of the church, singing in chorus as they went.

All these ceremonies had so claimed my attention that I had given scarcely any heed to the Virgin. She was seated humbly in the straw beside the little crib, in which still nestled the Bambino, and, with eyes cast down in maternal thoughtfulness, she was a lovely object there beneath the roof of the leafy stable. She did not appear to notice the actors in the drama; and now, when three young girls, in gayest holiday attire, came forward with distaffs that streamed with bright ribbons, and knelt before her, she reached forth a hand as if to bless them, but kept her eyes turned meekly upon the ground.

As these three girls retired from the manger, another and larger band appeared beneath the gallery opposite the shepherds, singing in sweet voices a salutation to the three who had just left the chancel. These made answer that they had come from the stable where the Saviour was born; and so, in alternate questions and answers, they described all that they had seen. The two groups, having advanced a step or two at each stanza, now met, and went back to the manger together, singing the same air the shepherds had previously sung.

When they arrived at the stable they made their offering, setting up a tent the while, ornamented with plenteous ribbons and flowers, among which blackbirds, thrushes, turtle-doves and partridges fluttered about at the ends of cords to which they were fastened. They brought with them, also, bunches of purple grapes and strings of yellow apples, chaplets of dried prunes and heaps of walnuts and chestnuts. After arranging these rustic offerings, the shepherdesses returned, singing in chorus as they went:

"In Bethlehem, at midnight, The Virgin mother bore her child. This world contains no fairer sight Than this fair Babe and Mary mild. Well may we sing at sight like this, *Gloria in Excelsis.*"

I now had another unobstructed view of Donna Isabella, and Jose Rosado's gossip, intensified by her romantic appearance as the Virgin, had given me a deep interest in her every movement.

She reached down into the little crib to lift out the Bambino, and I could plainly see a look of astonishment rise to her face as she started back, both hands held wide apart, as if having encountered something they were unprepared to touch. Then she turned hurriedly to Joseph and whispered a word in his ear, whereupon he too bent with surprise over the little crib. After gazing at it a moment, he reached down and lifted out, not the waxen Bambino, but a sweet young baby that smiled and reached its tiny arms from Joseph towards the white Virgin.

Donna Isabella was visibly affected at this, and took the tender infant into her arms, caressing and soothing it, while it fondled her face and white head-dress.

The audience had now become aware that, instead of the waxen image in the crib, there had been found a living baby, and the impetuous and susceptible minds of the Spanish peasants had jumped at the conclusion that they had witnessed a new miracle. They crowded up to the manger, telling their beads and murmuring prayers, while they pushed and jostled each other madly for a glimpse of the holy infant.

One of the acolytes reached his arms forth to take it from Donna Isabella and bring it to the chancel rail for the crowd to see, but she held it more closely to her bosom, and refused to let it go from her. As she stood there, a tall and stately figure, folded in the white gown of the Virgin and wearing the close head-dress which concealed all save her splendid face, she seemed the creation of some old painter, and the curious crowd of peasants was hushed into admiration by her beauty and her tenderness for the child. She, too, became a part of the strange miracle. The infant Christ had been born anew among them, and lay there in his very mother's arms, an object of mystery and worship. As the silence of wonder ensued, Donna Isabella seemed to collect her startled senses, and looked around her as if expecting the mother of the child to come and claim it. A woman of her resolution was not to be hurried into superstitious follies by some pretty trick or accident. But the little one lay so softly in her arms and reached with such tiny, appealing fingers at her throat, that she began to feel a motherly fondness for it. And, moreover, had it not been sent her, who was alone now in the great castle on the hill, as a mysterious gift of Providence? Ought she not to feel it a sacred charge, coming as it did, from the very manger, to her arms?

Thus thinking, the Donna Isabella came slowly to the chancel rail, and, holding forth the infant at arms' length, she said:

"Good people of Alcala, my part in the Christmas play is done. The good Lord has sent me this little one to take care of; and here, before you all, I accept the charge and promise to cherish and love it. If any of you know its mother, say that the Donna Isabella has carried it to the castle of Aranjuez, and tell her to follow it there, for where her child is, there the mother should be also." This broke the spell. The silent crowd fell into murmurs and gestures, and each one asked his neighbor where the child belonged. There was no longer any doubt. It was merely a human child; but the mystery of the manger surrounded it with a hallowed interest, and everybody was eager to discover its parents and bear them the good news of its adoption by the great lady.

Now, Jose Rosado was too old a hand, too jolly a host, to be long deceived. He whispered me his views as we stood near the leafy stable, and they were to the effect that the wayward son of the Aranjuez knew more about the child in the manger than any one else thereabouts.

And Jose was right; for, before the bustle of inquiry had quite died away, from out the sacristy door came a young girl wearing a veil and dressed in the long black gown of the Christmas ceremonies. She walked demurely through the crowd, which parted for her with inquiring looks, and, going straight up to the chancel, dropped on her knees before the Donna Isabella. She held down her head and made no motion; but all knew instinctively that she was the mother of the child.

The noble Virgin stooped and raised her head with a loving compassion. She put aside her veil and moved as if to kiss her, but one look at the mother's face turned her kindness into rage. She cried, "What, you?" and overwhelmed at the discovery sank down on the straw of the stable, clasping the child with a firmer hold, as if to shield it from a foe.

It was a sore conflict for an unyielding will like that of the Donna Isabella; but the part she had played in the sacred ceremonies and the surrounding emblems of peace and good-will were softening influences. More potent even than these was the persuasive contact of the little hands which opened and shut in playful touches at her throat. I could see from the varying expressions of her face that she questioned herself. Should she yield? The pride of birth, the disobedience of a youthful son to a mother of her indulgent nature, the stigma of a low connection upon a noble family name—all these things pleaded urgently, No. She looked up vindictively at the gaping congregation, which seemed spellbound in wanton curiosity, wherewith was mingled not a little religious dread. And then, again, she turned her eyes down upon the innocent face beside her bosom, so guileless, to be the cause of such varying passions in the throng about it. No, she could not give it up. All the old maternal instincts were aroused in her, and the firmness of her will was redoubled by the sentiment of love for her grandchild. Was it not her son's child, then, as well as this woman's? Surely, she had a right to keep it, and, glancing up with this last plea for possession on her lips, she saw beside the kneeling wife a new figure, whose presence made her pause and falter.

Only for an instant, however, for a kindlier light came into her clear eyes, and reaching forth the one arm which was free she threw it around her son's neck and kissed him fondly, while the little child which had wrought the change,—a latter-day miracle of broken affections made whole, of bitter wounds healed by the touch of innocence,—lay there between them, striving, with its playful hands, to catch at its mother's bowing head.

As Jose Rosado and I walked homeward through the pale-blue moonlight, we did not say much. I was deeply moved by the touching scene I had beheld; and he was exceedingly reflective.

At last, as we neared La Fonda's vine-run walls, he said:

"Señor, do you think the miracles are all over nowadays?"

"I know not, Señor Jose," I answered; "but there are certainly strange potencies lurking in the depths of a mother's love."

From a Cuirassier's Note-Book.

"He was a handsome fellow, the

son of a peasant; but he carried

his blue dolman very well, this

young soldier."

De Maupassant.

SALVETTE AND BERNADOU.

I.

It is the eve of Christmas in a large village of Bavaria. Along the snow-whitened streets, amid the confusion of the fog and noise of carriages and bells, the crowd presses joyously about cook-shops, wine-booths, and busy stores. Rustling with a light sweep of sound against the flower-twined and be-ribboned stalls, branches of green holly, or whole saplings, graced with pendants and shading the heads below like boughs of the Thuringian forest, go by in happy arms: a remembrance of nature in the torpid life of winter.

Day dies out. Far away, behind the gardens of the Résidence, lingers a glimmer of the departing sun, red in the fog; and in the town is such gaiety, such hurry of preparation for the holiday, that each jet of light which springs up in the many windows seems to hang from some vast Christmas-tree.

This is, in truth, no ordinary Christmas. It is the year of grace eighteen hundred and seventy, and the holy day is only a pretext the more to drink to the illustrious Von der Than and celebrate the triumph of the Bavarian troops.

"Noël, Noël!" The very Jews of the old town join in the mirth. Behold the aged Augustus Cahn who turns the corner by the "Blue Grapes!" Truly, his eyes have never shined before as they do to-night; nor has his little wicker satchel ever jingled so lightly. Across his sleeve, worn by the cords of sacks, is passed an honest little hamper, full to the top and covered with a cold napkin, from under which stick out the neck of a bottle and a twig of holly.

What on earth can the old miser want with all this? Can it be possible that he means to celebrate Christmas himself? Does he mean to have a family reunion and drink to the German fatherland? Impossible! Everybody knows old Cahn has no country. His fatherland is his strong box. And, moreover, he has neither family nor friends,—nothing but debtors. His sons and his associates are gone away long ago with the army. They traffic in the rear among the wagons, vending the water of life, buying watches, and, on nights of battle, emptying the pockets of the dead, or rifling the baggage tumbled in the ditches of the route.

Too old to follow his children, Father Cahn has remained in Bavaria, where he has made magnificent profits from the French prisoners of war. He is always prowling about the barracks to buy watches, shoulder-knots, medals, post-orders. You may see him glide through the hospitals, beside the ambulances. He approaches the beds of the wounded and demands, in a low, hideous growl,—

"Haf you anyting to sell?"

And, hold! At this same moment, the reason he trots so gayly with his basket under his arm, is solely that the military hospital closes at five o'clock, and that there are two Frenchmen who await him high up in that tall black building with straight, iron-barred windows, where Christmas finds nothing to welcome her approach save the pale lights which guard the pillows of the dying.

II.

These two Frenchmen are named Salvette and Bernadou. They are infantrymen from the same village of Provençe, enrolled in the same battalion, and wounded by the same shell. But Salvette had the stronger frame, and already he begins to grow convalescent, to take a few steps from his bed towards the window.

Bernadou, though, will never be cured. Through the pale curtains of the hospital bed, his figure looks more meagre, more languished day by day; and when he speaks of his home, of return thither, it is with that sad smile of the sick wherein there is more of resignation than of hope.

To-day, now, he is a little animated by the thought of the cheerful Christmas time, which, in our country of Provençe, is like a grand bonfire of joy lighted in the midst of winter; by remembrance of the departure for Mass at midnight; the church bedecked and luminous; the dark streets of the village full of people; then the long watch around the table; the three traditional flambeaux; the ceremony of the Yule-log; then the grand promenade around the house, and the sparkle of the burning wine.

"Ah, my poor Salvette, what a sad Christmas we are going to have this year! If only we had money to buy a little loaf of white bread and a flask of claret wine! What a pleasure it would be before passing away forever to sprinkle once again the Yule-log, with thee!"

And, in speaking of white bread and claret wine, the eyes of the sick youth glistened with pleasure.

But what to do? They had nothing, neither money nor watches. Salvette still held hidden in the seam of his mantle a post-order for forty francs. But that was for the day when they should be free and the first halt they should make in a cabaret of France. That was sacred; not to be touched!

But poor Bernadou is so sick. Who knows whether he will ever be able to return? And, then, it is Christmas, and they are together, perhaps, for the last time. Would it not be better to use it, after all?

Then, without a word to his comrade, Salvette loosens his tunic to take out the post-order, and when old Cahn comes, as he does every morning to make his tour of the aisles, after long debates and discussions under the breath, he thrusts into the Jew's hands the slip of paper, worn and yellow, smelling of powder and dashed with blood.

From that moment Salvette assumed an air of mystery. He rubbed his hands and laughed all to himself when he looked at Bernadou. And, as night fell, he was on the watch, his forehead pressed eagerly against the window-pane, until he saw, through the fog of the deserted court below, old Augustus Cahn, who came panting with his exertions, and carrying a little basket on his arm.

III.

This solemn midnight, which sounds from all the bells of the town, falls sadly into the pale night of the sick. The hospital is silent, lit only by the night-lamps suspended from the ceiling. Great running shadows flit over the beds and bare walls in a perpetual balancing, which seems to image the heavy respiration of all the sufferers lying there.

At times, dreamers talk high in their feverish sleep, or groan in the clutches of nightmares; while from the street there mounts up a vague rumor of feet and voices, mingled in the cold and sonorous night like sounds made under a cathedral porch.

Salvette feels the gathering haste, the mystery of a religious feast crossing the hours of sleep, the hanging forth in the dark village of the blind light of lanterns and the illumination of the windows of the church.

"Are you asleep, Bernadou?"

Softly, on the little table next his comrade's bed, Salvette has placed a bottle of *vin de Lunel* and a loaf of bread, a pretty Christmas loaf, where the twig of holly is planted straight in the centre.

Bernadou opens his eyes encircled with fever. By the indistinct glow of the night-lamps and under the white reflection of the great roofs where the moonlight lies dazzlingly on the snow, this improvised Christmas feast seems but a fantastic dream.

The Hospital

"Come, arouse thee, comrade! It shall not be said that two sons of Provençe have let this midnight pass without sprinkling a drop of claret!" And Salvette lifts him up with the tenderness of a mother. He fills the goblets, cuts the bread, and then they drink and talk of Provençe.

Little by little Bernadou grows animated and moved by the occasion,—the white wine, the remembrances! With that child-like manner which the sick find in the depths of their feebleness he asks Salvette to sing a Provençal Noël. His comrade asks which: "The Host," or "The Three Kings," or "St. Joseph Has Told Me"?

"No; I like the 'Shepherds' best. We chant that always at home."

"Then, here's for the 'Shepherds.'"

And in a low voice, his head between the curtains, Salvette began to sing.

All at once, at the last couplet, when the shepherds, coming to see Jesus in His stable, have placed in the manger their offerings of fresh eggs and cheeses, and when, bowing with an affable air,

"Joseph says, 'Go! be very sage:Return, and make you good voyage,Shepherds,Take your leave!'"

—all at once poor Bernadou slipped and fell heavily on the pillow. His comrade thought he had fallen asleep, and called him, shook him. But the wounded boy rested immovable, and the little twig of holly lying across the rigid cloth, seemed already the green palm they place upon the pillows of the dead.

Salvette understood at last. Then, in tears, a little weakened by the feast and by his grief, he raised in full voice, through the silence of the room, the joyous refrain of Provençe,—

"Shepherds,Take your leave!"

A Breton Peasant's Romance.

"Eyes dark; face thin, long, and

sallow; nose aquiline, but not

straight, having a peculiar inclination

towards the left cheek;

expression, therefore, sinister."

Dickens.

THE WOLF TOWER.

I.

Long ago, in Brittany, under the government of St. Gildas the Wise, seventh abbot of Ruiz, there lived a young tenant of the abbey who was blind in the right eye and lame in the left leg. His name was Sylvestre Ker, and his mother, Josserande Ker, was the widow of Martin Ker, in his lifetime the keeper of the great door of the Convent of Ruiz.

The mother and the son lived in a tower, the ruins of which are seen at the foot of Mont Saint Michel de la Trinité, in the grove of chestnut-trees that belongs to Jean Maréchal, the mayor's nephew. These ruins are now called the Wolf Tower, and the Breton peasants shudder as they pass through the chestnut-grove; for at midnight, around the Wolf Tower, and close to the first circle of great stones erected by the Druids at Carnac, are seen the phantoms of a young man and a young girl—Pol Bihan and Matheline du Coat-Dor.

The young girl is of graceful figure, with long, floating hair, but without a face; and the young man is tall and robust, but the sleeves of his coat hang limp and empty, for he is without arms.

Round and round the circle they pass in opposite directions, and, strange to tell, they never meet, nor do they ever speak to each other.

Once a year, on Christmas night, instead of walking they run; and all the Christians who cross the heath to go to the midnight Mass hear from afar the young girl cry,—

"Wolf Sylvestre Ker, give me back my beauty!" and the deep voice of the young man adds, "Wolf Sylvestre Ker, give me back my strength!"

II.

And this has lasted for thirteen hundred years; therefore you may well think there is a story connected with it.

When Martin Ker, the husband of Dame Josserande, died, their son Sylvestre was only seven years old. The widow was obliged to give up the guardianship of the great door to a man-at-arms, and retire to the tower, which was her inheritance; but little Sylvestre Ker had permission to follow the studies in the convent school.

The boy showed natural ability, but he studied little except in the class of chemistry, taught by an old monk named Thaël, who was said to have discovered the secret of making gold out of lead by adding to it a certain substance which no one but himself knew; for certainly, if the fact had been communicated, all the lead in the country would have been quickly turned into gold.

As for Thaël himself, he had been careful not to profit by his secret, for Gildas the Wise had once said to him,—

"Thaël, Thaël, God does not wish you to change the work of His hands. Lead is lead, and gold is gold. There is enough gold, and not too much lead. Leave God's works alone; if not, Satan will be your master."

Most assuredly such precepts would not be well received by modern industry; but St. Gildas knew what he said, and Thaël died of extreme old age before he had changed the least particle of lead into gold. This, however, was not from want of will, which was proved after his death, as the rumor spread about that Thaël did not altogether desert his laboratory, but at times returned to his beloved labors. Many a time, in the lonely hours of the night, the fishermen, in their barks, watched the glimmer of the light in his former cell; and Gildas the Wise, having been warned of the fact, arose one night before Lauds, and with quiet steps crossed the corridors, thinking to surprise his late brother, and perhaps ask of him some details of the other side of the dreaded door which separates life from death.

When he reached the cell he listened, and heard Thaël's great bellows puffing and blowing, although no one had yet been appointed to succeed him. Gildas suddenly opened the door with his master-key, and saw before him little Sylvestre Ker actively employed in relighting Thaël's furnaces.

St. Gildas was not a man to give way to sudden wrath; he took the child by the ear, drew him outside, and said to him, gently,—

"Ker, my little Ker, I know what you are attempting and what tempts you to make the effort; but God does not wish it, nor I either, my little Ker."

"I do it," replied the boy, "because my dear mother is so poor."

"Your mother is what she is; she has what God gives her. Lead is lead and gold is gold. If you go against the will of God, Satan will be your master."

Little Ker returned to the tower crestfallen, and never again slipped into the cell of the dead Thaël; but when he was eighteen years old a modest inheritance was left him, and he bought materials for dissolving metals and distilling the juice of plants. He gave out that his aim was to learn the art of healing; for that great purpose he read great books which treated of medical science and many other things besides.

He was then a youth of fine appearance, with a noble, frank face, neither one-eyed nor lame, and led a retired life with his mother, who ardently loved her only son.

No one visited them in the tower except the laughing Matheline, the heiress of the tenant of Coat-Dor and god-daughter of Josserande; and Pol Bihan, son of the successor of Martin Ker as armed keeper of the great door.

Both Pol and Matheline often conversed together, and upon what subject do you think? Always of Sylvestre Ker. Was it because they loved him? No. What Matheline loved most was her own fair self, and Pol Bihan's best friend was named Pol Bihan.

Matheline passed long hours before her little mirror of polished steel, which faithfully reflected her laughing mouth full of pearls; and Pol was proud of his great strength, for he was the best wrestler in the Carnac country. When they spoke of Sylvestre Ker, it was to say, "What if some fine morning he should find the secret of the fairy-stone that is the mother of gold!"

And each one mentally added,—

"I must continue to be friendly with him, for if he becomes wealthy he will enrich me."

Josserande also knew that her beloved son sought after the fairy-stone, and even had mentioned it to Gildas the Wise, who shook his venerable head and said,—

"What God wills will be. Be careful that your son wears a mask over his face when he seeks the cursed thing; for what escapes from the crucible is Satan's breath, and the breath of Satan causes blindness."

Josserande, meditating upon these words, went to kneel before the cross of St. Cado, which is in front of the seventh stone of Cæsar's camp,—the one that a little child can move by touching it with his finger, but that twelve horses harnessed to twelve oxen cannot stir from its solid foundation. Thus prostrate, she prayed: "O Lord Jesus! Thou who hast mercy for mothers on account of the Holy Virgin, Thy mother, watch well over my little Sylvestre, and take from his head this thought of making gold. Nevertheless, if it is Thy will that he should be rich, Thou art the Master of all things, my sweet Saviour!"

And as she rose she murmured: "What a beautiful boy he would be with a cloak of fine cloth and a hood bordered with fur, if he only had means to buy them."

III.

It came to pass that as all these young people, Pol Bihan, Matheline, and Sylvestre Ker, gained a year each time that twelve months rolled by, they reached the age to think of marriage; and Josserande, one morning, proceeded to the dwelling of the farmer of Coat-Dor to ask the hand of Matheline for her son, Sylvestre Ker; at which proposal Matheline opened her rosy mouth so wide, to laugh the louder, that far back she showed two pearls which had never before been seen.

When her father asked her if the offer suited her, she replied, "Yes, father and godmother, provided that Sylvestre Ker gives me a gown of cloth of silver embroidered with rubies, like that of the Lady of Lannelar, and that Pol Bihan may be our groomsman."

Pol, who was there, also laughed, and said, "I will assuredly be groomsman to my friend Sylvestre Ker, if he consents to give me a velvet mantle striped with gold, like that of the Castellan of Gâvre, the Lord of Carnac."

Whereupon Josserande returned to the tower, and said to her son, "Ker, my darling, I advise you to choose another friend and another bride; for those two are not worthy of your love."

But the young man began to sigh and groan, and answered, "No friendship or love will I ever know except for Pol, my dear comrade, and Matheline, your god-daughter, my beautiful playfellow."

And Josserande having told him of the two new pearls that Matheline had shown in the back of her mouth, nothing would do but he must hurry to Coat-Dor to try and see them, also.

On the road from the tower to the farm of Coat-Dor is the Point of Hinnic, where the grass is salt, which makes the cows and rams very fierce while they are grazing.

As Sylvestre Ker walked down the path at the end of which is the Cross of St. Cado, he saw, on the summit of the promontory, Pol and Matheline strolling along, talking and laughing; so he thought,—

"I need not go far to see Matheline's two pearls."

And, in fact, the girl's merry laughter could be heard below, for it always burst forth if Pol did but open his lips. When, lo, and behold! a huge old ram, which had been browsing on the salt grass, tossed back his two horns, and, fuming at the nostrils, bleated as loud as the stags cry when chased, and rushed in the direction of Matheline's voice; for, as every one knows, the rams become furious if laughter is heard in their meadow.

He ran quickly, but Sylvestre Ker ran still faster, and arrived the first by the girl, so that he received the shock of the ram's butting while protecting her with his body. The injury was not very great, only his right eye was touched by the curved end of one of the horns when the ram raised his head, and thus Sylvestre Ker became one-eyed.

The ram, prevented from slaughtering Matheline, dashed after Pol Bihan, who fled; reached him just at the end of the cliff, and pushed him into the sea, that beat against the rocks fifty feet below.

Well content with his work, the ram walked off, and the legend says he laughed behind his woolly beard.

But Matheline wept bitterly, and cried,—

"Ker, my handsome Ker, save Bihan, your sweet friend, from death, and I pledge my faith I will be your wife without any condition."

At the same time, amid the roaring of the waves, was heard the imploring voice of Pol Bihan crying,—

"Sylvestre, O Sylvestre Ker! my only friend, I cannot swim. Come quickly and save me from dying without confession, and all you may ask of me you shall have, were it the dearest treasure of my heart."

Sylvestre Ker asked,—

"Will you be my groomsman?" And Bihan replied,—

"Yes, yes; and I will give you a hundred crowns. And all that your mother may ask of me she shall have. But hasten, hasten, dear friend, or the waves will carry me off."

Sylvestre Ker's blood was pouring from the wound in his eye, and his sight was dimmed; but he was generous of heart, and boldly leaped from the top of the promontory. As he fell, his left leg was jammed against a jutting rock and broke, so there he was, lame as well as one-eyed; nevertheless, he dragged Bihan to the shore and asked,—

"When shall the wedding be?"

As Matheline hesitated in her answer—for Sylvestre's brave deeds were too recent to be forgotten—Pol Bihan came to her assistance and gayly cried,—

"You must wait, Sylvestre, my saviour, until your leg and eye are healed."

"Still longer," added Matheline (and now Sylvestre Ker saw the two new pearls, for in her laughter she opened her mouth from ear to ear); "still longer, as limping, one-eyed men are not to my taste—no, no!"

"But," cried Sylvestre Ker, "it is for your sakes that I am one-eyed and lame."

"That is true," said Bihan.

"That is true," also repeated Matheline, for she always spoke as he did.

"Ker, my friend Ker," resumed Bihan, "wait until to-morrow, and we will make you happy."

And off they went, Matheline and he, arm-in-arm, leaving Sylvestre to go hobbling along to the tower, alone with his sad thoughts.

Would you believe it? Trudging wearily home, he consoled himself by thinking he had seen two new pearls behind the smile. You may, perhaps, think you have never met such a fool. Undeceive yourself; it is the same with all the men, who only look for laughing girls with teeth like pearls. But the sorrowful one was Josserande, the widow, when she saw her son with only one eye and one sound leg.

"Where did all this happen," she asked, with tears.

And as Sylvestre Ker gently answered, "I have seen them, mother; they are very beautiful," Josserande divined that he spoke of her god-daughter's two pearls, and cried,—

"By all that is holy, he has also lost his mind!"

Then seizing her staff, she went to the Abbey of Ruiz to consult St. Gildas as to what could be done in this unfortunate case. And the wise man replied,—

"You should not have spoken of the two pearls; your son would have remained at home. But, now that the evil is done, nothing will happen to him contrary to God's holy will. At high tide the sea comes foaming over the sands, yet see how quietly it retires. What is Sylvestre Ker doing now?"

"He is lighting his furnaces," replied Josserande.

The wise man paused to reflect, and after a little while said,—

"In the first place, you must pray devoutly to the Lord our God, and afterwards look well before you to know where to put your feet. The weak buy the strong, the unhappy the happy; did you know that, my good woman? Your son will persevere in search of the fairy-stone that changes lead into gold, to pay for Pol's wicked friendship and for the pearls behind the dangerous smiles of that Matheline. Since God permits it, all is right. Yet see that your son is well protected against the smoke of his crucible, for it is the very breath of Satan; and make him promise to go to the midnight Mass."

For it was near the glorious Feast of Christmas.

IV.

Josserande had no difficulty in making Sylvestre Ker promise to go to the midnight Mass, for he was a good Christian; and she bought for him an iron armor to put on when he worked around his crucibles, so as to preserve him from Satan's breath.

And it happened that, late and early, Pol Bihan now came to the tower, bringing with him the laughing Matheline; for it was rumored that at last Sylvestre Ker would soon find the fairy-stone and become a wealthy man.

It was not only two new pearls that Matheline showed at the corners of her rosy mouth, but a brilliant row that shone, and chattered, and laughed, from her lips down to her throat; for Pol

Bihan had said to her: "Laugh as much as you can; for smiles attract fools, as the turning mirror catches larks."

We have spoken of Matheline's lips, of her throat, and of her smile, but not of her heart; of that we can only say the place where it should have been was nearly empty; so she replied to Bihan,—

"As much as you will. I can afford to laugh to be rich; and when the fool shall have given me all the gold of the earth, all the pleasures of the world, I will be happy, happy.... I will have them all for myself, for myself alone, and I will enjoy them."

Pol Bihan clasped his hands in admiration, so lovely and wise was she for her age; but he thought: "I am wiser still than you, my beauty; we will share between us what the fool will give—one-half for me, and the other also; the rest for you. Let the water run under the bridge."

The day before Christmas they came together to the tower,— Matheline carrying a basket of chestnuts, Pol a large jug, full of sweet cider,—to make merry with the godmother.

They roasted the chestnuts in the ashes, heated the cider before the fire, adding to it fermented honey, wine, sprigs of rosemary, and marjoram leaves; and so delicious was the perfume of the beverage that even Dame Josserande longed for a taste.

On the way thither, Pol had advised Matheline adroitly to question Sylvestre Ker, to know when he would at last find the fairy-stone.

Sylvestre Ker neither ate chestnuts nor drank wine, so absorbed was he in the contemplation of Matheline's bewitching smiles; and she said to him,—

"Tell me, my handsome, lame, and one-eyed bridegroom, will I soon be the wife of a wealthy man?"

Sylvestre Ker, whose eye shot forth lurid flame, replied,—

"You would have been as rich as you are beautiful to-morrow, without fail, if I had not promised my dear mother to accompany her to the midnight Mass to-night. The favorable hour falls just at the first stroke of Matins."

"To-day?"

"Between to-day and to-morrow."

"And can it not be put off?"

"Yes, it can be put off for seven years."

Dame Josserande heard nothing, as Pol was relating an interesting story, so as to distract her attention; but, while talking, he listened with all his ears.

Matheline laughed no longer, and thought,—

"Seven years! Can I wait seven years?" Then she continued:

"Beautiful bridegroom, how do you know that the propitious moment falls precisely at the hour of Matins? Who told you so?"

"The stars," replied Sylvestre Ker. "At midnight Mars and Saturn will arrive in diametrical opposition; Venus will seek Vesta; Mercury will disappear in the sun; and the planet without a name, that the deceased Thaël divined by calculation, I saw last night, steering its unknown route through space to come in conjunction with Jupiter. Ah! if I only dared disobey my dear mother." He was interrupted by a distant vibration of the bells of Plouharnel, which rang out the first signal of the midnight Mass.

Josserande instantly left her wheel.

"It would be a sin to spin one thread more," said she. "Come, my son Sylvestre, put on your Sunday clothes, and let us be off for the parish church, if you please."

Sylvestre wished to rise, for never yet had he disobeyed his mother; but Matheline, seated at his side, detained him and murmured in silvery tones,—

"My handsome friend, you have plenty of time."

Pol, on his side, said to Dame Josserande,—

"Get your staff, neighbor, and start at once, so as to take your time. Your god-daughter Matheline will accompany you; and I will follow with friend Sylvestre, for fear some accident might happen to him with his lame leg and sightless eye." As he proposed, so it was done; for Josserande suspected nothing, knowing that her son had promised, and that he would not break his word.

As they were leaving, Pol whispered to Matheline,—

"Amuse the good woman well, for the fool must remain here."

And the girl replied,—

"Try and see the caldron in which our fortune is cooking. You will tell me how it is done."

Off the two women started; a large, kind mother's heart full of tender love, and a sparrow's little gizzard, narrow and dry, without enough room in it for one pure tear. For a moment Sylvestre Ker stood on the threshold of the open door to watch them depart. On the gleaming white snow their two shadows fell—the one bent and already tottering, the other erect, flexible, and each step seemed a bound. The young lover sighed. Behind him, in a low voice, Pol Bihan said,—

"Ker, my comrade, I know what you are thinking about, and you are right to think so; this must come to an end. She is as impatient as you are, for her love equals yours; for both of you it is too long to wait."

Sylvestre Ker turned pale with joy.

"Do you speak truth?" he stammered. "Am I fortunate enough to be loved by her?"

"Yes, on my faith!" replied Pol Bihan; "she loves you too well for her own peace. When a girl laughs too much, it is to keep from weeping,—that's the real truth."

V.

Well might they call him "the fool," poor Sylvestre Ker! Not that he had less brains than another man,—on the contrary, he was now very learned—but love crazes him who places his affections on an unworthy object.

Sylvestre Ker's little finger was worth two dozen Pol Bihan's and fifty Matheline's; in spite of which Matheline and Pol Bihan were perfectly just in their contempt, for he who ascends the highest falls lowest.

When Sylvestre had re-entered the tower, Pol commenced to sigh heavily, and said,—

"What a pity! What a great, great pity!"

"What is a pity?" asked Sylvestre Ker.

"It is a pity to miss such a rare opportunity."

Sylvestre Ker exclaimed, "What opportunity? So you were listening to my conversation with Matheline?"

"Why, yes," replied Pol. "I always have an ear open to hear what concerns you, my true friend. Seven years! Shall I tell you what I think? You would only have twelve months to wait to go with your mother to another Christmas Mass."

"I have promised," said Sylvestre.

"That is nothing: if your mother loves you truly, she will forgive you."

"If she loves me!" cried Sylvestre Ker. "Oh, yes, she loves me with her whole heart."

Some chestnuts still remained, and Bihan shelled one while he said,—

"Certainly, certainly, mothers always love their children; but Matheline is not your mother. You are one-eyed, you are lame, and you have sold your little patrimony to buy your furnaces. Nothing remains of it. Where is the girl that can wait seven years? Nearly the half of her age!... If I were in your place, I would not throw away my luck as you are about to do, but at the hour of Matins I would work for my happiness."

Sylvestre Ker was standing before the fireplace. He listened, his eyes bent down, with a frown upon his brow.

"You have spoken well," at last he said; "my dear mother will forgive me. I shall remain, and will work at the hour of Matins."

"You have decided for the best!" cried Bihan. "Rest easy; I will be with you in case of danger. Open the door of your laboratory. We will work together; I will cling to you like your shadow!"

Sylvestre Ker did not move, but looked fixedly upon the floor, and then, as if thinking aloud, murmured,—

"It will be the first time I have ever caused my dear mother sorrow!"

He opened a door, but not that of the laboratory, pushed Pol Bihan outside, and said,—

"The danger is for myself alone; the gold will be for all. Go to the Christmas Mass in my place; say to Matheline that she will be rich, and to my dear mother that she will have a happy old age, since she will live and die with her fortunate son."

VI.

When Sylvestre Ker was alone, he listened to the noise of the waves dashing upon the beach and the sighing of the wind among the great oaks,—two mournful sounds. And he looked with conflicting feelings at the empty seats of Matheline and of his dear mother Josserande. Little by little had he seen the black hair of the widow become gray, then white, around her sunken temples. That night memory carried him back even to his cradle, over which had bent the sweet, noble face of her who had always spoken to him of God.

But whence came those golden ringlets that mingled with Josserande's black hair, and which shone in the sunlight above his mother's snowy locks? And that laugh, oh! that silvery laugh of youth, which prevented Sylvestre Ker from hearing, in his pious recollections, the calm, grave voice of his mother. Whence did it come?

Seven years! Pol had said. "Where is the girl who can wait seven years?" and these words floated in the air. Never had the son of Martin Ker heard such strange voices amid the roaring of the ocean, nor in the rushing winds of the forest of the Druids.

Suddenly the tower also commenced to speak, not only through the cracks of the old windows where the mournful wind sighed, but with a confusion of sounds that resembled the busy whispering of a crowd, that penetrated through the closed doors of the laboratory, under which a bright light streamed. Sylvestre Ker opened the door, fearing to see all in a blaze, but there was no fire; the light that streamed under the door came from the round, red eye of his furnace, and happened to strike the stone of the threshold. No one was in the laboratory; still, the noises, similar to the chattering of an audience awaiting a promised spectacle, did not cease. The air was full of speaking things; the spirits could be felt swarming around, as closely packed as the wheat in the barn or the sand on the seashore. And, although not seen, they spoke all kinds of phantom-words, which were heard right and left, before and behind, above and below, and which penetrated through the pores of the skin like quicksilver passing through a cloth.

They said,—

"The Magi has started, my friend."

"My friend, the Star shines in the East."

"My friend, my friend, the little King Jesus is born in the manger, upon the straw."

"Sylvestre Ker will surely go with the shepherds."

"Not at all; Sylvestre Ker will not go."

"Good Christian he was."

"Good Christian he is no longer."

"He has forgotten the name of Joseph."

"And the name of Mary."

"No, no, no!"

"Yes, yes, yes!"

"He will go!"

"He will not go!"

"He will go, since he promised Dame Josserande."

"He will not go, since Matheline told him to stay."

"My friend, my friend, to-night Sylvestre Ker will find the golden secret."

"To-night, my friend, my friend, he will win the heart of the one he loves."

And the invisible spirits, thus disputing, sported through the air, mounting, descending, whirling around like atoms of dust in a sunbeam, from the flag-stones of the floor to the rafters of the roof.

Inside the furnace, in the crucible, some other thing responded, but it could not be well heard, as the crucible had been hermetically sealed.

"Go out from here, you wicked crowd," cried Sylvestre Ker, sweeping around with a broom of holly branches. "What are you doing here? Go outside, cursed spirits, damned souls—go, go!"

From all the corners of the room came laughter; Matheline seemed everywhere. Suddenly there was profound silence, and the wind from the sea brought the sound of the bells of Plouharnel, ringing the second peal for the midnight Mass.

"My friend, what are they saying?"

"They say Christmas, my friend—Christmas, Christmas, Christmas!"

"Not at all! They say, Gold, gold, gold!"

"You lie, my friend!"

"My friend, you lie!"

And the other voices, those that were grumbling in the interior of the furnace, swelled and puffed.

The fire, that no person was blowing, kept up by itself, hot as the soul of a forge should be. The crucible became red, and the stones of the furnace were dyed a deep scarlet.

In vain did Sylvestre Ker sweep with his holly broom; between the branches, covered with sharp leaves, the spirits passed,—nothing could catch them; and the heat was so great the boy was bathed in perspiration.

After the bells had finished their second peal, he said,—

"I am stifling. I will open the window to let out the heat as well as this herd of evil spirits."

But as soon as he opened the window, the whole country commenced to laugh under its white mantle of snow—barren heath, ploughed land, Druid stones, even to the enormous oaks of the forest, with their glistening summits, that shook their frosty branches, saying,—

"Sylvestre Ker will go! Sylvestre Ker will not go!"

Not a spirit from within flew out, while all the outside spirits entered, muttering, chattering, laughing,—

"Yes, yes, yes, yes! No, no, no, no!" And I believe they fought.

At the same time the sound of a cavalcade advancing was heard on the flinty road that passed before the tower; and Sylvestre Ker recognized the long procession of the monks of Ruiz, led by the grand abbot, Gildas the Wise, arrayed in cope and mitre, with his crozier in his hand, going to the Mass of Plouharnel, as the convent chapel was being rebuilt.

When the head of the cavalcade approached the tower, the grand abbot cried out,—

"My armed guards, sound your horns to awaken Dame Josserande's son!"

And instantly there was a blast from the horns, which rang out until Gildas the Wise exclaimed,—

"Be silent, for there is my tenant wide awake at his window."

When all was still, the grand abbot raised his crozier and said,—

"My tenant, the first hour of Christmas approaches, the glorious Feast of the Nativity. Extinguish your furnaces and hasten to Mass, for you have barely time." And on he passed, while those in the procession, as they saluted Ker, repeated,—

"Sylvestre Ker, you have barely time; make haste!"

The voices of the air kept gibbering: "He will go! He will not go!" and the wind whistled in bitter sarcasm.

Sylvestre Ker closed his window. He sat down, his head clasped by his trembling hands. His heart was rent by two forces that dragged him, one to the right, the other to the left,—his Mother's prayer and Matheline's laughter.

He was no miser; he did not covet gold for the sake of gold, but that he might buy the row of pearls and smiles that hung from the lips of Matheline....

"Christmas!" cried a voice in the air.

"Christmas, Christmas, Christmas!" repeated all the other voices.

Sylvestre Ker suddenly opened his eyes, and saw that the furnace was fiery red from top to bottom, and that the crucible was surrounded with rays so dazzling he could not even look at it. Something was boiling inside that sounded like the roaring of a tempest.

"Mother! Oh, my dear mother!" cried the terrified man, "I am coming. I'll run...."

But thousands of little voices stung his ears with the words,—

"Too late, too late, too late! It is too late!"

Alas! alas! the wind from the sea brought the third peal of the bells of Plouharnel, and they also said to him: "Too late."

VII.

As the sound of the bells died away, the last drop of water fell from the clepsydra and marked the hour of midnight. Then the furnace opened and showed the glowing crucible, which burst with a terrible noise, and threw out a gigantic flame that reached the sky through the torn roof. Sylvestre Ker, enveloped by the fire, fell prostrate on the ground, suffocated in the burning smoke.

The silence of death followed. Suddenly an awful voice said to him: "Arise." And he arose.

On the spot where had stood the furnace, of which not a vestige remained, was standing a man, or rather a colossus; and Sylvestre Ker needed but a glance to recognize in him the demon. His body appeared to be of iron, red-hot and transparent; for in his veins could be seen the liquid gold, flowing into, and then retreating from, his heart, black as an extinguished coal.

The creature, who was both fearful and beautiful to behold, extended his hand towards the side of the tower nearest the sea, and in the thick wall a large breach was made.

"Look!" said Satan.

Sylvestre Ker obeyed. He saw, as though distance were annihilated, the interior of the humble church of Plouharnel where the faithful We assembled. The officiating priest had just ascended the altar, brilliant with the Christmas candles, and there was great pomp and splendor; for the many monks of Gildas the Wise were assisting the poor clergy of the parish.

In a corner, under the shadow of a column knelt Dame Josserande in fervent prayer, but often did the dear woman turn towards the door to watch for the coming of her son.

Not far from her was Matheline du Coat-Dor, bravely attired and very beautiful, but lavishing the pearls of her smiles upon all who sought them, forgetting no one but God; and, close to Matheline, Pol Bihan squared his broad shoulders. Then, even as Satan had given to Sylvestre Ker's sight the power of piercing the walls, so did he permit him to look into the depth of hearts. In his mother's heart he saw himself as in a mirror. It was full of him. Good Josserande prayed for him; she prayed to Jesus, whose feast is Christmas, in the pious prayer which fell from her lips; and ever and ever said her heart to God: "My son, my son, my son!"

In the heart of Pol, Sylvestre Ker saw pride of strength and gross cupidity; in the spot where should have been the heart of Matheline, he saw Matheline, and nothing but Matheline, in adoration before Matheline.

"I have seen enough," said Sylvestre Ker.

"Then," replied Satan, "listen!" And immediately the sacred music resounded in the ears of the young tenant of the tower as plainly as though he was in the church of Plouharnel. They were singing the Sanctus: "Holy, holy, holy, Lord God of Hosts! The heavens and the earth are full of Thy glory. Hosanna in the highest! Blessed is He that cometh in the name of the Lord. Hosanna in the highest!"

Dame Josserande repeated the words with the others, but the refrain of her heart continued: "O Jesus, Infinite Goodness! may he be happy. Deliver him from all evil, from all sin. I have only him to love.... Holy, holy, holy, give me all the suffering and keep for him all the happiness!"

Can you believe it? Even while piously inhaling the perfume of this celestial hymn, the young tenant wished to know what Matheline was saying to God. Everything speaks to God,—the wild beasts in the forest, the birds in the air, even the plants, whose roots are in the ground.

But miserable girls who sell the pearls of their smiles are lower than the animals and vegetables. Nothing is beneath them,—Pol Bihan excepted. Instead of speaking to God, Pol Bihan and Matheline whispered together, and Sylvestre Ker heard them as distinctly as if he had been between them.

"How much will the fool give?" asked Matheline.

"The idiot will give you all," replied Pol.

"And must I really squint with that one-eyed creature, and limp with the lame wretch?"

Sylvestre Ker felt his heart die away within him.

Meanwhile, Josserande prayed earnestly for Sylvestre Ker.

"Never mind," continued Bihan; "it is worth while limping and squinting for a time to win all the money in the world."

"That is true; but for how long?"

Sylvestre Ker held his breath to hear the better.

"As long as you please," answered Pol Bihan.

There was a pause, after which the gay Matheline resumed in a lower tone,—

"But ... they say after a murder one can never laugh, and I wish to laugh always...."

"Will I not be there?" replied Bihan. "Some time or other the idiot will certainly seek a quarrel with me, and I will crack his bones by only squeezing him in my arms; you can count upon my strength."

"I have heard enough," said Sylvestre Ker to Satan.

"And do you still love this Bihan?"

"No: I despise him."

"And Matheline,—do you love her yet?"

"Yes, oh! yes!... but ... I hate her!"

"I see," said Satan, "that you are a coward, and wicked like all men. Since you have heard and seen enough at a distance, listen, and look at your feet...."

The wall closed with a loud crash of the stones as they came together, and Sylvestre Ker saw that he was surrounded by an enormous heap of gold-pieces, as high as his waist, which gently floated, singing the symphony of riches. All around him was gold, and through the gap in the roof the shower of gold fell, and fell, and fell.

"Am I the master of all this?" asked Sylvestre Ker.

"Yes," replied Satan; "you have compelled me, who am gold, to come forth from my caverns; you are therefore the master of gold, provided you purchase it at the price of your soul. You cannot have both God and gold. You must choose one or the other."

"I have chosen," said Sylvestre Ker. "I keep my soul."

"You have firmly decided?"

"Irrevocably."

"Once, twice, ... reflect! You have just acknowledged that you still love the laughing Matheline."

"And that I hate her.... Yes, ... it is so.... But in eternity I wish to be with my dear mother, Josserande."

"Were there no mothers," growled Satan, "I could play my game much better in the world!"

And he added,—

"For the third time, ... adjudged!"

The heap of gold became as turbulent as the water of a cascade, and leaped and sang; the millions of little sonorous coins clashed against each other, and then all was silent and they vanished.

The room appeared as black as a place where there had been a fire; nothing could be seen but the lurid gleam of Satan's iron body. Then said Sylvestre Ker,—

"Since all is ended, retire!"

VIII.

But the demon did not stir.

"Do you think, then," he asked, "that you have brought me hither for nothing? There is the law. You are not altogether my slave, since you have kept your soul; but as you have freely called me, and I have come, you are my vassal. I have a half claim over you. The little children know that; I am astonished at your ignorance.... From midnight to three o'clock in the morning you belong to me, in the form of an animal, restless, roving, complaining, without help from God. This is what you owe to your strong friend and beautiful bride. Let us settle the affair before I depart. What animal do you wish to be,—roaring lion, bellowing ox, bleating sheep, crowing cock? If you become a dog, you can crouch at Matheline's feet, and Bihan can lead you by a leash to hunt in the woods...."

"I wish," cried Sylvestre Ker, whose anger burst forth at these words, "I wish to be a wolf, to devour them both!"

"So be it," said Satan; "wolf you shall be three hours of the night during your mortal life.... Leap, wolf!"

And the wolf, Sylvestre Ker, leaped, and with one dash shattered the casement of the window as he cleared it with a bound. Through the aperture in the roof Satan escaped, and, spreading a pair of immense wings, rapidly disappeared in an opposite direction from the steeple of Plouharnel, whose chimes were ringing across the snow.

IX.

I do not know if you have ever seen a Breton village come forth after the midnight Mass. It is a joyous sight, but a brief one, as all are in a hurry to return home, where the midnight meal awaits them,—a frugal feast, but eaten with such cheerful hearts. The people, for a moment massed in the cemetery, exchange hospitable invitations, kind wishes, and friendly jokes; then divide into little caravans, which hurry along the roads, laughing, talking, singing. If it is a clear, cold night, the clicking of their wooden shoes may be heard for some time; but if it is damp weather, the sound is stifled, and after a few moments the faint echo of an "adieu" or Christmas greeting is all that can be heard around the church as the beadle closes it.

In the midst of all this cheerfulness Josserande alone returned with a sad heart; for through the whole Mass she had in vain watched for her beloved son. She walked fifty paces behind the cavalcade of the monks of Ruiz, and dared not approach the Grand Abbot Gildas, for fear of being questioned about her boy. On her right was Matheline du Coat-Dor, on her left Bihan,—both eager to console her; for they thought that by that time Sylvestre Ker must have learned the wonderful secret which would secure him untold wealth, and to possess the son they should cling to the mother; therefore there were promises and caresses, and "will you have this, or will you have that?"

"Dear godmother, I shall always be with you," said Matheline, "to comfort and rejoice your old age; for your son is my heart."

Pol Bihan continued,—

"I will never marry, but always remain with my friend, Sylvestre Ker, whom I love more than myself. And nothing must worry you; if he is weak, I am strong, and I will work for two."

To pretend that Dame Josserande paid much attention to all these words would be false; for her son possessed her whole soul, and she thought,—

"This is the first time he has ever disobeyed and deceived me. The demon of avarice has entered into him. Why does he want so much money? Can all the riches in the world pay for one of the tears that the ingratitude of a beloved son draws from his mother's eyes?"

Suddenly her thoughts were arrested, for the sound of a trumpet was heard in the still night.

"It is the convent horn," said Matheline.

"And it sounds the wolf-alarm," added Pol.

"What harm can the wolf do," asked Josserande, "to a well-mounted troop like the cavalry of Gildas the Wise? And, besides, cannot the holy abbot with a single word put to flight a hundred wolves?"

They arrived at the heath of Carnac, where are the two thousand seven hundred and twenty-nine Druid stones, and the monks had already passed the round point where nothing grows, neither grass nor heath, and which resembles an enormous caldron,—a caldron wherein to make oaten-porridge,—or rather a race-course, to exercise horses.

On one side might be seen the town, dark and gloomy; on the other, as far as the eye could reach, rows of rugged obelisks, half-black, half-white, owing to the snow, which threw into bold relief each jagged outline. Josserande, Matheline, and Pol Bihan had just turned from the sunken road which branches towards Plouharnel; and the moon played hide-and-go-seek behind a flock of little clouds that flitted over the sky like lambs.

Then a strange thing happened. The cavalcade of monks was seen to retreat from the entrance of the avenues to the middle of the circle, while the horn sounded the signal of distress, and loud cries were heard of "Wolf! wolf! wolf!" At the same time could be distinguished the clashing of arms, the stamping of horses, and all the noise of a ferocious struggle, above which rose the majestic tones of Gildas the Wise, as he said, with calmness,—

"Wolf, wicked wolf, I forbid you to touch God's servants!" But it seemed that the wicked wolf was in no hurry to obey, for the cavalcade plunged hither and thither as though shaken by convulsion; and the moon having come forth from the clouds, there was seen an enormous beast struggling with the staffs of the monks, the halberds of the armed guard, the pitchforks and spears of the peasants, who had hastened from all directions at the trumpet-call from Ruiz.

The animal received many wounds, but it was fated not to die. Again and again it charged upon the crowd, rushed up and down, round and round, biting, tearing with its great teeth so fearfully that a large circle was made around the grand abbot, who was finally left alone in face of the wolf. For a wolf it was. And the grand abbot having touched it with his crosier, the wolf crouched at his feet, panting, trembling, and bloody.

Gildas the Wise bent over it, looked at it attentively, then said,—

"Nothing happens contrary to God's will. Where is Dame Josserande?"

"I am here," replied a mournful voice full of tears, "and I dread a great misfortune."

She also was alone; for Matheline and Pol Bihan, seized with terror, had rushed across the fields at the first alarm and abandoned their precious charge. The grand abbot called Josserande and said,—

"Woman, do not despair. Above you is the Infinite Goodness, who holds in His hands the heavens and the whole earth.

Meanwhile, protect your wolf; we must return to the monastery to gain from sleep strength to serve the Lord our God!"

And he resumed his course, followed by his escort.

The wolf did not move; his tongue lay on the snow, which was reddened by his blood. Josserande knelt beside him and prayed fervently. For whom? For her beloved son. Did she already know that the wolf was Sylvestre Ker? Certainly; such a thing could scarcely be divined; but under what form cannot a mother discover her darling child?

She defended the wolf against the peasants, who had returned to strike him with their pitchforks and pikes, as they believed him dead. The two last who came were Pol Bihan and Matheline. Pol Bihan kicked him on the head, and said, "Take that, you fool!" and Matheline threw stones at him, and cried: "Idiot, take that, and that, and that!"

They had hoped for all the gold in the world, and this dead beast could give them nothing more.

After a while two ragged beggars passed by and assisted Josserande in carrying the wolf into the tower. Where is charity most often found? Among the poor, who are the figures Of Jesus Christ.

X.

Day dawned. A man slept in the bed of Sylvestre Ker, where widow Josserande had laid a wolf. The room still bore the marks of a fire, and snow fell through the hole in the roof. The young tenant's face was disfigured with blows, and his hair, stiffened with blood, hung in heavy locks. In his feverish sleep he talked, and the name that escaped his lips was Matheline's. At his bedside the mother watched and prayed.

When Sylvestre Ker awoke he wept, for the thought of his condemnation returned; but the remembrance of Pol and Matheline dried the tears in his burning eyes.

"It was for those two," said he, "that I forgot God and my mother. I still feel my friend's heel upon my forehead, and even to the bottom of my heart the shock of the stones thrown at me by my betrothed!"

"Dearest," murmured Josserande, "dearer to me than ever, I know nothing; tell me all."

Sylvestre Ker obeyed, and when he had finished, Josserande kissed him, took up her staff, and proceeded towards the convent of Ruiz to ask, according to her custom, aid and counsel from Gildas the Wise. On the way, men, women, and children looked curiously at her, for throughout the country it was already known that she was the mother of a wolf. Even behind the hedge which enclosed the abbey orchard Matheline and Pol were hidden to see her pass; and she heard Pol say,—

"Will you come to-night to see the wolf run around?"

"Without fail," replied Matheline; and the sting of her laughter pierced Josserande like a poisonous thorn.

The grand abbot received her, surrounded by great books and dusty manuscripts. When she wished to explain her son's case, he stopped her, and said,—

"Widow of Martin Ker, poor, good woman, since the beginning of the world, Satan, the demon of gold and pride, has worked many such wickednesses. Do you remember the deceased brother, Thaël, who is a saint for having resisted the desire of making gold,—he who had the power to do it?"

"Yes," answered Josserande; "and would to heaven my Sylvestre had imitated him!"

"Very well," replied Gildas the Wise. "Instead of sleeping, I passed the rest of the night with St. Thaël, seeking a means to save your son, Sylvestre Ker."

"And have you found it, father?"

The grand abbot neither answered yes nor no, but he began to turn over a very thick manuscript filled with pictures; and, while turning the leaves, he said,—

"Life springs from death, according to the divine word; death seizes the living, according to the pagan law of Rome; and it is nearly the same thing in the order of miserable temporal ambition, whose inheritance is a strength, a life, shot forth from a coffin. This is a book of the defunct Thaël's, which treats of the question of maladies caused by the breath of gold,—a deadly poison.... Woman, would you have the courage to strike your wolf a blow on his head powerful enough to break the skull?"

At these words Josserande fell her full length upon the tiles, as if she had been stabbed to the heart; but in the very depth of her agony—for she thought herself dying—she replied,—

"If you should order me to do it, I would."

"You have this great confidence in me, poor woman?" cried Gildas, much moved.

"You are a man of God," answered Josserande, "and I have faith in God."

Gildas the Wise prostrated himself on the ground and struck his breast, knowing that he had felt a movement of pride. Then, standing up, he raised Josserande, and kissed the hem of her robe, saying,—

"Woman, I adore you in the most holy faith. Prepare your axe, and sharpen it!"

XI.

In the days of Gildas the Wise, intense silence always reigned at night through the dense oak forest of the Armorican country. One of the most lonely places was Cæsar's camp, the name was given to the huge masses of stone that encumbered the barren heath; and it was the common opinion that the pagan giants, supposed to be buried under them, rose from their graves at midnight and roamed up and down the long avenues, watching for the late passers-by, to twist their necks.

This night, however,—the night after Christmas,—many persons could be seen, about eleven o'clock, on the heath before the stones of Carnac, all around the Great Basin or circle, whose irregular outline was clearly visible by moonlight. The enclosure was entirely empty. Outside no one was seen, it is true; but many could be heard gabbling in the shadow of the high rocks, under the shelter of the stumps of oaks, even in the tufts of thorny brambles; and all this assemblage watched for something, and that something was the wolf, Sylvestre Ker. They had come from Plouharnel, and also from Lannelar, from Carnac, from Kercado, even from the old town of Crach, beyond La Trinité.

Who had brought together all these people, young and old, men and women? The legend does not say; but very probably Matheline had strewn around the cruel pearls of her laughter, and Pol Bihan had not been slow to relate what he had seen after the midnight Mass.

By some means or other, the entire country around for five or six leagues knew that the son of Martin Ker, the tenant of the abbey, had become a man-wolf, and that he was doomed to expiate his crime in the spot haunted by the phantoms,—the Great Basin of the Pagans, between the tower and the Druid stones.

Many of the watchers had never seen a man-wolf, and there reigned in the crowd, scattered in invisible groups, a fever of curiosity, terror, and impatience; the minutes lengthened as they passed, and it seemed as though midnight, stopped on the way, would never come.

There were at that time no clocks in the neighborhood to mark the hour, but the matin-bell of the convent of Ruiz gave notice that the wished-for moment had arrived.

While waiting there was busy conversation: they spoke of the man-wolf, of phantoms, and also of betrothals, for the rumor was spread that the bans of Matheline du Coat-Dor, the promised bride of Sylvestre Ker, with the strong Pol Bihan, who had never found a rival in the wrestling-field, would be published on the following Sunday; and I leave you to imagine how Matheline's laughter ran in pearly cascades when congratulated on her approaching marriage.

By the road which led up to the tower a shadow slowly descended; it was not the wolf, but a poor woman in mourning, whose head was bent upon her breast, and who held in her hand an object that shone like a mirror, and the brilliant surface of which reflected the moonbeams.

"It is Josserande Ker!" was whispered around the circle, behind the rocks, in the brambles, and under the stumps of the oaks.

"'Tis the widow of the armed keeper of the great door!"

"'Tis the mother of the wolf, Sylvestre Ker!"

"She also has come to see...."

"But what has she in her hand?"

Twenty voices asked the question. Matheline, who had good eyes, and such beautiful ones, replied,—

"It looks like an axe.... Happy am I to be rid of those two, the mother and son! With them I could never laugh."

But there were two or three good souls who said in low tones,—

"Poor widow! her heart must be full of sorrow."

"But what does she want with that axe?"

"It is to defend her wolf," again replied Matheline, who carried a pitchfork.

Pol Bihan held an enormous hollow stick which resembled a club. Every one was armed either with threshing-flails or rakes or hoes; some even bore scythes, carried upright; for they had not only come to look on, but to make an end of the man-wolf.

Again was heard the chime of the matin-bells of the convent of Ruiz, and immediately a smothered cry ran from group to group,—

"Wolf! wolf! wolf!"

Josserande heard it, for she paused in her descent and cast an anxious look around; but, seeing no one, she raised her eyes to heaven and clasped her hands over the handle of her axe.

The wolf, in the meantime, with fuming nostrils and eyes which looked like burning coals, leaped over the stones of the enclosure and began to run around the circle.

"See, see!" said Pol Bihan; "he no longer limps." And Matheline, dazzled by the red light from his eyes, added: "It seems he is no longer one-eyed!"

Pol brandished his club, and continued,—

"What are we waiting for? Why not attack him?"

"Go you first," said the men.

"I caught cold the other day, and my leg is stiff, which keeps me from running," answered Pol.

"Then I will go first!" cried Matheline, raising her pitchfork. "I will soon show how I hate the wretch!"

Dame Josserande heard her, and sighed,—

"Girl, whom I blessed in baptism, may God keep me from cursing you now!"

This Matheline, whose pearls were worth nothing, was no coward; for she carried out her words, and marched straight up to the wolf, while Bihan stayed behind and cried,—

"Go, go, my friends; don't be afraid! Ah! but for my stiff leg, I would soon finish the wolf, for I am the strongest and bravest."

Round and round the circle galloped the wolf as quickly as a hunted stag; his eyes darted fire, his tongue was hanging from his mouth. Josserande, seeing the danger that threatened him, wept and cried out,—

"O Bretons! is there among you all not one kind soul to defend the widow's son in the hour when he bitterly expiates his sin?"

"Let us alone, godmother," boldly replied Matheline.

And from afar Pol Bihan added: "Don't listen to the old woman; go!"

But another voice was heard in answer to Dame Josserande's appeal, and it said,—

"As last night, we are here!"

Standing in front of Matheline and barring the passage were two ragged beggars, with their wallets, leaning upon their staffs. Josserande recognized the two poor men who had so charitably aided her the night before; and one of them, who had snow-white hair and beard, said,—

"My brethren, why do you interfere in this? God rewards and punishes. This poor man-wolf is not a damned soul, but one expiating a great crime. Leave justice to God, if you do not wish some great misfortune to happen to you."

And Josserande, who was kneeling down, said imploringly,—

"Listen, listen to the saint!"

But from behind, Pol Bihan cried out,—

"Since when have beggars been allowed to preach sermons? Ah! if it were not for my stiff leg.... Kill him, kill him!... wolf! wolf!"

"Wolf! wolf!" repeated Matheline, who tried to drive off the old beggar with her pitchfork. But the fork broke like glass in her hands as it touched the poor man's tatters, and at the same time twenty voices cried,—

"The wolf! the wolf! Where has the wolf gone?"

Soon it was seen where the wolf had gone. A black mass dashed through the crowd, and Pol Bihan uttered a horrible cry,—

"Help! help! Matheline!"

You have often heard the noise made by a dog when crunching a bone. This was the noise they heard, but louder, as though there were many dogs crunching many bones. And a strange voice, like the growling of a wolf, said,—

"The strength of a man is a dainty morsel for a wolf to eat. Bihan, traitor, I eat your strength!"

The black mass again bounded through the terrified crowd, his bloody tongue hanging from his mouth, his eyes darting fire.

This time it was from Matheline that a scream still more horrible than that of Pol's was heard; and again there was the noise of another terrible feast, and the voice of the wild beast, which had already spoken, growled,—

"The pearls of a smile make a dainty morsel for a wolf to eat. Matheline, serpent that stung my heart, seek for your beauty. I have eaten it!"

XII.

The white-haired beggar had endeavored to protect Matheline against the wolf, but he was very old, and his limbs would not move as quickly as his heart. He only succeeded in throwing down the wolf. It fell at Josserande's feet and licked her knees, uttering doleful moans. But the people, who had come thither for entertainment, were not well pleased with what had happened. There was now abundance of light, as men with torches had arrived from the abbey in search of Gildas the Wise, whose cell had been found empty at the hour of Compline.

The glare from the torches shone upon two hideous wounds made by the wolf, who had devoured Matheline's beauty and Pol's strength,—that is to say, the face of the one and the arms of the other—flesh and bones. It was frightful to behold. The women wept while looking at the repulsive, bleeding mass which had been Matheline's smiling face; the men sought in the double bloody gaps some traces of Pol's arms, for the powerful muscles, the glory of the athletic games; and every heart was filled with wrath.

And the legend says that the tenant of Coat-Dor, Matheline's poor father, knelt beside his daughter and felt around in the blood for the scattered pearls, which were now as red as holly-berries.

"Alas!" said he, "of these dead, stained things, which when living were so beautiful, which were admired and envied and loved, I was so proud and happy."

Alas! indeed, alas! Perhaps it was not the girl's fault that her heart was no larger than a little bird's; and yet for this defect was not Matheline cruelly punished?

"Death to the wolf! death to the wolf! death to the wolf!"

From all sides was this cry heard, and brandishing pitchforks, cudgels, ploughshares, and mallets, came rushing the people towards the wolf, who still lay panting, with open jaws and pendent tongue, at the feet of Dame Josserande.

Around them the torch-bearers formed a circle: not to throw light upon the wolf and Dame Josserande, but to render homage to the white-haired beggar, in whom, as though the scales had suddenly fallen from their eyes, every one recognized the Grand Abbot of Ruiz, Gildas the Wise.

The grand abbot raised his hand, and the armed crowd's eager advance was checked, as if their feet had been nailed to the ground. Calmly he surveyed them, blessed them, and said,—

"Christians, the wolf did wrong to punish, for chastisement belongs to God alone; therefore the wolf's fault should not be punished by you. In whom resides the power of God? In the holy authority of fathers and mothers. So here is my penitent Josserande, who will rightfully judge the wolf and punish him; she is his mother."

When Gildas the Wise ceased speaking, you could have heard a mouse run across the heath. Each one thought to himself: "So the wolf is really Sylvestre Ker." But not a word was uttered, and all looked at Dame Josserande's axe, which glistened in the moonlight.

Josserande's heart sank within her, and she murmured,—

"My beloved one, my beloved one, whom I have borne in my arms and nourished with my milk,—ah! me, can the Lord God inflict this cruel martyrdom upon me?"

No one replied, not even Gildas the Wise, who silently adjured the All-Powerful, and recalled to Him the sacrifice of Abraham.

Josserande raised her axe, but she had the misfortune to look at the wolf, who fixed his eyes, full of tears, upon her, and the axe fell from her hands.

It was the wolf who picked it up, and when he gave it back to her, he said,—

"I weep for you, my mother."

"Strike!" cried the crowd; for what remained of Pol and Matheline uttered terrible groans. "Strike! strike!"

While Josserande again seized her axe, the grand abbot had time to say,—

"Do not complain, you two unhappy ones; for your suffering here below changes your hell into heaven."

Three times Josserande raised the axe, three times she let it fall without striking; but at last she said, in a hoarse tone that sounded like a death-rattle, "I have great faith in the good God!" and then she struck boldly, for the wolf's head split in two halves.

XIII.

A sudden wind extinguished the torches, and some one prevented Dame Josserande from falling, as she sank fainting to the ground, by supporting her in his arms.

By the light of the halo which shone around the blessed head of Gildas the Wise, the good people saw that this somebody was the young tenant, Sylvestre Ker, no longer lame and one-eyed, but with two straight legs and two perfect eyes.

At the same time there were heard voices in the clouds chanting. And why? Because heaven and earth quivered with emotion at witnessing this supreme act of faith soaring from the depth of anguish in a mother's heart.

XIV.

This is the legend that for many centuries has been related at Christmas-time on the shores of the Petite-Mer, which, in the Breton tongue, is called Armor bihan, the Celtic name of Brittany.

If you ask what moral these good people draw from this strange story, I will answer that it contains a basketful. Pol and Matheline, condemned to walk around the Basin of the Pagans until the end of time,—one without arms, the other without a face,—offer a severe lesson to those who are too proud of their broad shoulders and brute force, and gossiping flirts of girls with smiling faces and wicked hearts; the case of Sylvestre Ker teaches young men not to listen to the demon of money; the blow of Josserande's axe shows the miraculous power of faith.

Still further, that you may bind together these diverse morals in one, here is a proverb which is current in the province: "Never stoop to pick up the pearls of a smile." After this, ask me no more.

As to the authenticity of the story, I have already said that the chestnut-grove belongs to the mayor's nephew, which is one guarantee; and I will add that the spot is called Sylvestre-ker, and that the ruins hung with moss have no other name than "The Wolf Tower."

An Indian Officer's Idyll.

"An officer and a gentleman—which

is an enviable thing."

Kipling.

THE PEACE EGG.

I.

Every one ought to be happy at Christmas. But there are many things which ought to be, and yet are not; and people are sometimes sad even in the Christmas holidays.

The Captain and his wife were sad, though it was Christmas Eve. Sad, though they were in the prime of life, blessed with good health, devoted to each other and to their children, with competent means, a comfortable house on a little freehold property of their own, and, one might say, everything that heart could desire. Sad, though they were good people, whose peace of mind had a firmer foundation than their earthly goods alone; contented people, too, with plenty of occupation for mind and body. Sad—and in the nursery this was held to be past all reason—though the children were performing that ancient and most entertaining play or Christmas Mystery of Good St. George of England, known as "The Peace Egg," for their benefit and behoof alone.

The play was none the worse that most of the actors were too young to learn parts, so that there was very little of the rather tedious dialogue, only plenty of dress and ribbons, and of fighting with wooden swords. But though St. George looked bonny enough to warm any father's heart, as he marched up and down with an air learned by watching many a parade in barrack-square and drill-ground, and though the Valiant Slasher did not cry in spite of falling hard and the Doctor treading accidentally on his little finger in picking him up, still the Captain and his wife sighed nearly as often as they smiled, and the mother dropped tears as well as pennies into the cap which the King of Egypt brought round after the performance.

II.

Many, many years back the Captain's wife had been a child herself, and had laughed to see the village mummers act "The Peace Egg," and had been quite happy on Christmas Eve. Happy, though she had no mother. Happy, though her father was a stern man, very fond of his only child, but with an obstinate will that not even she dared thwart. She had lived to thwart it, and he had never forgiven her. It was when she married the Captain. The old man had a prejudice against soldiers, which was quite reason enough, in his opinion, for his daughter to sacrifice the happiness of her future life by giving up the soldier she loved. At last he gave her her choice between the Captain and his own favor and money. She chose the Captain, and was disowned and disinherited.

The Captain bore a high character, and was a good and clever officer, but that went for nothing against the old man's whim. He made a very good husband, too; but even this did not move his father-in-law, who had never held any intercourse with him or his wife since the day of their marriage, and who had never seen his own grandchildren. Though not so bitterly prejudiced as the old father, the Captain's wife's friends had their doubts about the marriage. The place was not a military station, and they were quiet country folk who knew very little about soldiers, while what they imagined was not altogether favorable to "red-coats," as they called them.

Soldiers are well-looking generally, it is true, and the Captain was more than well-looking—he was handsome; brave, of course it is their business, and the Captain had V. C. after his name and several bits of ribbon on his patrol jacket. But then, thought the good people, they are here to-day and gone to-morrow, you "never know where you have them;" they are probably in debt, possibly married to several women in several foreign countries, and, though they are very courteous in society, who knows how they treat their wives when they drag them off from their natural friends and protectors to distant lands, where no one can call them to account?

"Ah, poor thing!" said Mrs. John Bull, junior, as she took off her husband's coat on his return from business, a week after the Captain's wedding, "I wonder how she feels? There's no doubt the old man behaved disgracefully; but it's a great risk marrying a soldier. It stands to reason, military men aren't domestic; and I wish—Lucy Jane, fetch your papa's slippers, quick!—she'd had the sense to settle down comfortably among her friends with a man who would have taken care of her."

"Officers are a wild set, I expect," said Mr. Bull, complacently, as he stretched his limbs in his own particular arm-chair, into which no member of his family ever intruded. "But the red-coats carry the day with plenty of girls who ought to know better. You women are always caught by a bit of finery. However, there's no use our bothering our heads about it. As she has brewed she must bake."

The Captain's wife's baking was lighter and more palatable than her friends believed. The Captain, who took off his own coat when he came home, and never wore slippers but in his dressing-room, was domestic enough.

A selfish companion must, doubtless, be a great trial amid the hardships of military life, but when a soldier is kind-hearted, he is often a much more helpful and thoughtful and handy husband than any equally well-meaning civilian. Amid the ups and downs of their wanderings, the discomforts of shipboard and of stations in the colonies, bad servants, and unwonted sicknesses, the Captain's tenderness never failed. If the life was rough, the Captain was ready. He had been, by turns, in one strait or another, sick-nurse, doctor, carpenter, nursemaid, and cook to his family, and had, moreover, an idea that nobody filled these offices quite so well as himself. Withal, his very profession kept him neat, well-dressed, and active. In the roughest of their ever-changing quarters he was a smarter man, more like the lover of his wife's young days, than Mr. Bull amid his stationary comforts.

Then if the Captain's wife was—as her friends said—"never settled," she was also forever entertained by new scenes; and domestic mischances do not weigh very heavily on people whose possessions are few and their intellectual interests many.

It is true that there were ladies in the Captain's regiment who passed by sea and land from one quarter of the globe to another, amid strange climates and customs, strange trees and flowers, beasts and birds, from the glittering snow of North America to the orchids of the Cape, from beautiful Pera to the lily-covered hills of Japan, and who in no place rose above the fret of domestic worries, and had little to tell on their return but of the universal misconduct of servants, from Irish "helps" in the colonies to *compradors* and China-boys at Shanghai. But it was not so with the Captain's wife. Moreover, one becomes accustomed to one's fate, and she moved her whole establishment from the Curragh to Corfu with less anxiety than that felt by Mrs. Bull over a port-wine stain on the best table-cloth.

And yet, as years went and children came, the Captain and his wife grew tired of travelling. New scenes were small comfort when they heard of the death of old friends. One foot of murky English sky was dearer, after all, than miles of the unclouded heavens of the South. The gray hills and overgrown lanes of her old home haunted the Captain's wife by night and day, and homesickness, that weariest of all sicknesses, began to take the light out of her eyes before their time. It preyed upon the Captain, too. Now and then he would say, fretfully, "I should like an English resting-place, however small, before everybody is dead! But the children's prospects have to be considered." The continued estrangement from the old man was an abiding sorrow also, and they had hopes that, if only they could get to England, he might be persuaded to peace and charity this time.

At last they were sent home. But the hard old father still would not relent. He returned their letters unopened. This bitter disappointment made the Captain's wife so ill that she almost died, and in one month the Captain's hair became iron gray. He reproached himself for having ever taken the daughter from her father, "to kill her at last," as he said. And, thinking of his own children, he even reproached himself for having robbed the old widower of his only child. After two years at home his regiment was ordered to India. He failed to effect an exchange, and they prepared to move once more,—from Chatham to Calcutta. Never before had the packing, to which she was so well accustomed, been so bitter a task to the Captain's wife.

It was at the darkest hour of this gloomy time that the Captain came in, waving above his head a letter which changed all their plans.

Now close by the old home of the Captain's wife there had lived a man, much older than herself, who yet had loved her with a devotion as great as that of the young Captain. She never knew it, for, when he saw that she had given her heart to his young rival, he kept silence, and he never asked for what he knew he might have had—the old man's authority in his favor. So generous was the affection which he could never conquer, that he constantly tried to reconcile the father to his children while he lived, and, when he died, he bequeathed his house and small estate to the woman he had loved.

"It will be a legacy of peace," he thought, on his death-bed. "The old man cannot hold out when she and her children are constantly in sight. And it may please God that I shall know of the reunion I have not been permitted to see with my eyes."

And thus it came about that the Captain's regiment went to India without him, and that the Captain's wife and her father lived on opposite sides of the same road.

III.

The eldest of the Captain's children was a boy. He was named Robert, after his grandfather, and seemed to have inherited a good deal of the old gentleman's character, mixed with gentler traits. He was a fair, fine boy, tall and stout for his age, with the Captain's regular features, and, he flattered himself, the Captain's firm step and martial bearing. He was apt—like his grandfather—to hold his own will to be other people's law, and happily for the peace of the nursery this opinion was devoutly shared by his brother Nicholas. Though the Captain had sold his commission, Robert continued to command an irregular force of volunteers in the nursery, and never was a colonel more despotic. His brothers and sisters were by turn infantry, cavalry, engineers, and artillery, according to his whim, and when his affections finally settled upon the Highlanders of "The Black Watch," no female power could compel him to keep his stockings above his knees, or his knickerbockers below them.

The Captain alone was a match for his strong-willed son.

"If you please, sir," said Sarah, one morning, flouncing in upon the Captain, just as he was about to start for the neighboring town, "if you please, sir, I wish you'd speak to Master Robert. He's past my powers."

"I've no doubt of it," thought the Captain; but he only said, "Well, what's the matter?"

"Night after night do I put him to bed," said Sarah, "and night after night does he get up as soon as I'm out of the room, and says he's orderly officer for the evening, and goes about in his night-shirt and his feet as bare as boards."

The Captain fingered his heavy moustache to hide a smile, but he listened patiently to Sarah's complaints.

"It ain't so much him I should mind, sir," she continued, "but he goes round the beds and wakes up the other young gentlemen and Miss Dora, one after another, and when I speak to him he gives me all the sauce he can lay his tongue to, and says he's going round the guards. The other night I tried to put him back in his bed, but he got away and ran all over the house, me hunting him everywhere, and not a sign of him, till he jumps out on me from the garret-stairs and nearly knocks me down. 'I've visited the outposts, Sarah,' says he; 'all's well,' and off he goes to bed as bold as brass."

"Have you spoken to your mistress?" asked the Captain.

"Yes, sir," said Sarah. "And misses spoke to him, and he promised not to go round the guards again."

"Has he broken his promise?" asked the Captain, with a look of anger and also surprise.

"When I opened the door last night, sir," continued Sarah, in her shrill treble, "what should I see in the dark but Master Robert a-walking up and down with the carpet-brush stuck in his arm. 'Who goes there?' says he. 'You owdacious boy!' says I. 'Didn't you promise your ma you'd leave off them tricks?' 'I'm not going round the guards,' says he; 'I promised not. But I'm for sentry-duty to-night.' And say what I would to him, all he had for me was, 'You mustn't speak to a sentry on duty.' So I says, 'As sure as I live till morning, I'll go to your pa,' for he pays no more attention to his ma than me, nor to any one else."

"Please to see that the chair-bed in my dressing-room is moved into your mistress's bed-room," said the Captain. "I will attend to Master Robert."

With this Sarah had to content herself, and she went back to the nursery. Robert was nowhere to be seen, and made no reply to her summons. On this the unwary nursemaid flounced into the bed-room to look for him, when Robert, who was hidden beneath a table, darted forth and promptly locked her in.

"You're under arrest," he shouted through the keyhole.

"Let me out!" shrieked Sarah.

"I'll send a file of the guard to fetch you to the orderly-room by-and-by," said Robert, "for 'preferring frivolous complaints,'" and he departed to the farmyard to look at the ducks.

That night, when Robert went up to bed, the Captain quietly locked him into his dressing-room, from which the bed had been removed.

"You're for sentry-duty to-night," said the captain, "The carpet-brush is in the corner. Good-evening."

As his father anticipated, Robert was soon tired of the sentry game in these new circumstances, and long before the night had half worn away he wished himself safely undressed and in his own comfortable bed. At half-past twelve o'clock he felt as if he could bear it no longer, and knocked at the Captain's door.

"Who goes there?" said the Captain.

"Mayn't I go to bed, please?" whined poor Robert.

"Certainly not," said the Captain. "You're on duty."

And on duty poor Robert had to remain, for the Captain had a will as well as his son. So he rolled himself up in his father's railway rug and slept on the floor.

The next night he was glad to go quietly to bed, and remain there.

IV.

The Captain's children sat at breakfast in a large, bright nursery. It was the room where the old bachelor had died, and now *her* children made it merry. This is just what he would have wished.

They all sat round the table, for it was breakfast-time. There were five of them, and five bowls of boiled bread-and-milk smoked before them. Sarah, a foolish, gossiping girl, who acted as nurse till better could be found, was waiting on them, and by the table sat Darkie, the black retriever, his long, curly back swaying slightly from the difficulty of holding himself up, and his solemn hazel eyes fixed very intently on each and all of the breakfast bowls. He was as silent and sagacious as Sarah was talkative and empty-headed. The expression of his face was that of King Charles I. as painted by Vandyke. Though large, he was unassuming. Pax, the pug, on the contrary, who came up to the first joint of Darkie's leg, stood defiantly on his dignity and his short stumps. He always placed himself in front of the bigger dog, and made a point of hustling him in door-ways and of going first down stairs. He strutted like a beadle, and carried his tail more tightly curled than a bishop's crook. He looked as one may imagine the frog in the fable would have looked had he been able to swell himself rather nearer to the size of the ox. This was partly due to his very prominent eyes, and partly to an obesity favored by habits of lying inside the fender, and of eating meals proportioned more to his consequence than to his hunger. They were both favorites of two years' standing, and had very nearly been given away, when the good news came of an English home for the family, dogs and all.

Robert's tongue was seldom idle, even at meals. "Are you a Yorkshire woman, Sarah?" he asked, pausing, with his spoon full in his hand.

"No, Master Robert," said Sarah.

"But you understand Yorkshire, don't you? I can't, very often; but mamma can, and can speak it, too. Papa says mamma always talks Yorkshire to servants and poor people. She used to talk Yorkshire to Themistocles, papa said, and he said it was no good; for, though Themistocles knew a lot of languages, he didn't know that. And mamma laughed, and said she didn't know she did. Themistocles was our man-servant in Corfu," Robin added, in explanation. "He stole lots of things, Themistocles did; but papa found him out."

Robin now made a rapid attack on his bread-and-milk, after which he broke out again,—

"Sarah, who is that tall gentleman at church, in the seat near the pulpit? He wears a cloak like what the Blues wear, only all blue, and is tall enough for a Life-guardsman. He stood when we were kneeling down, and said, 'Almighty and most merciful Father,' louder than anybody."

Sarah knew who the old gentleman was, and knew also that the children did not know, and that their parents did not see fit to tell them as yet. But she had a passion for telling and hearing news, and would rather gossip with a child than not gossip at all. "Never you mind, Master Robin," she said, nodding sagaciously. "Little boys aren't to know everything."

"Ah, then, I know you don't know," replied Robert; "if you did, you'd tell. Nicholas, give some of your bread to Darkie and Pax. I've done mine. For what we have received, the Lord make us truly thankful. Say your grace, and put your chair away, and come along. I want to hold a court-martial." And, seizing his own chair by the seat, Robin carried it swiftly to its corner. As he passed Sarah, he observed, tauntingly, "You pretend to know, but you don't."

"I do," said Sarah.

"You don't," said Robin.

"Your ma's forbid you to contradict, Master Robin," said Sarah; "and if you do, I shall tell her. I know well enough who the old gentleman is, and perhaps I might tell you, only you'd go straight off and tell again."

"No, no, I wouldn't!" shouted Robin. "I can keep a secret; indeed, I can! Pinch my little finger, and try. Do, do tell me, Sarah; there's a dear Sarah, and then I shall know you know." And he danced round her, catching at her skirts.

To keep a secret was beyond Sarah's powers.

"Do let my dress be, Master Robin," she said; "you're ripping out all the gathers, and listen while I whisper. As sure as you're a living boy, that gentleman's your own grandpapa."

Robin lost his hold on Sarah's dress; his arm fell by his side, and he stood with his brows knit, for some minutes, thinking. Then he said, emphatically,—

"What lies you do tell, Sarah!"

"Oh, Robin!" cried Nicholas, who had drawn near, his thick curls standing stark with curiosity; "mamma said 'lies' wasn't a proper word, and you promised not to say it again."

"I forgot," said Robin. "I didn't mean to break my promise. But she does tell—ahem!—you know what."

"You wicked boy!" cried the enraged Sarah; "how dare you say such a thing, and everybody in the place knows he's your ma's own pa."

"I'll go and ask her," said Robin, and he was at the door in a moment; but Sarah, alarmed by the thought of getting into a scrape herself, caught him by the arm.

"Don't you go, love; it'll only make your ma angry. There; it was all my nonsense."

"Then it's not true?" said Robin, indignantly. "What did you tell me so for?"

"It was all my jokes and nonsense," said the unscrupulous Sarah. "But your ma wouldn't like to know I've said such a thing. And Master Robert wouldn't be so mean as to tell tales, would he, love?"

"I'm not mean," said Robin, stoutly; "and I don't tell tales; but you do, and you tell—you know what—besides. However, I won't go this time; but I'll tell you what,—if you tell tales of me to papa any more, I'll tell him what you said about the old gentleman in the blue cloak." With which parting threat Robin strode off to join his brothers and sister.

Sarah's tale had put the court-martial out of his head, and he leaned against the tall fender, gazing at his little sister, who was tenderly nursing a well-worn doll. Robin sighed.

"What a long time that doll takes to wear out, Dora!" said he. "When will it be done?"

"Oh, not yet, not yet!" cried Dora, clasping the doll to her, and turning away. "She's quite good, yet."

"How miserly you are," said her brother; "and selfish, too; for you know I can't have a military funeral till you'll let me bury that old thing."

Dora began to cry.

"There you go, crying!" said Robin, impatiently. "Look here: I won't take it till you get the new one on your birthday. You can't be so mean as not to let me have it then!"

But Dora's tears still fell. "I love this one so much," she sobbed. "I love her better than the new one."

"You want both; that's it," said Robin, angrily. "Dora, you're the meanest girl I ever knew!"

At which unjust and painful accusation Dora threw herself and her doll upon their faces, and wept bitterly. The eyes of the soft-hearted Nicholas began to fill with tears, and he squatted down before her, looking most dismal. He had a fellow-feeling for her attachment to an old toy, and yet Robin's will was law to him.

"Couldn't we make a coffin, and pretend the body was inside?" he suggested.

"No, we couldn't," said Robin. "I wouldn't play the 'Dead March' after an empty candle-box. It's a great shame,—and I promised she should be chaplain in one of my night-gowns, too."

"Perhaps you'll get just as fond of the new one," said Nicholas, turning to Dora.

But Dora only cried, "No, no! He shall have the new one to bury, and I'll keep my poor, dear, darling Betsey." And she clasped Betsey tighter than before.

"That's the meanest thing you've said yet," retorted Robin; "for you know mamma wouldn't let me bury the new one." And, with an air of great disgust, he quitted the nursery.

V.

Nicholas had sore work to console his little sister, and Betsey's prospects were in a very unfavorable state, when a diversion was caused in her favor by a new whim which put the military funeral out of Robin's head.

After he left the nursery he strolled out of doors, and, peeping through the gate at the end of the drive, he saw a party of boys going through what looked like a military exercise with sticks and a good deal of stamping; but instead of mere words of command, they all spoke by turns, as in a play. In spite of their strong Yorkshire accent, Robin overheard a good deal, and it sounded very fine.

Not being at all shy, he joined them, and asked so many questions that he soon got to know all about it. They were practising a Christmas mumming-play, called "The Peace Egg." Why it was called that they could not tell him, as there was nothing whatever about eggs in it, and, so far as its being a play of peace, it was made up of a series of battles between certain valiant knights and princes, of whom St. George of England was chief and conqueror. The rehearsal being over, Robin went with the boys to the sexton's house, (he was father to the "King of Egypt,") where they showed him the dresses they were to wear. These were made of gay-colored materials, and covered with ribbons, except that of the "Black Prince of Paradine," which was black, as became his title. The boys also showed him the book from which they learned their parts, and which was to be bought for one penny at the post-office shop.

"Then are you the mummers who come round at Christmas, and act in people's kitchens, and people give them money, that mamma used to tell us about?" said Robin.

St. George of England looked at his companions as if for counsel as to how far they might commit themselves, and then replied, with Yorkshire caution, "Well, I suppose we are."

"And do you go out in the snow from one house to another at night; and, oh, don't you enjoy it?" cried Robin.

"We like it well enough," St. George admitted.

Mummers

Robin bought a copy of "The Peace Egg." He was resolved to have a nursery performance, and to act the part of St. George himself. The others were willing for what he wished, but there were difficulties.

In the first place, there are eight characters in the play, and there were only five children. They decided among themselves to leave out the "Fool," and mamma said that another character was not to be acted by any of them, or, indeed, mentioned; "the little one who comes in at the end," Robin explained. Mamma had her reasons, and these were always good. She had not been altogether pleased that Robin had bought the play. It was a very old thing, she said, and very queer; not adapted for a child's play.

If mamma thought the parts not quite fit for the children to learn, they found them much too long; so, in the end, she picked out some bits for each, which they learned easily, and which, with a good deal of fighting, made quite as good a story of it as if they had done the whole. What may have been wanting otherwise was made up for by the dresses, which were charming.

Robin was St. George, Nicholas the Valiant Slasher, Dora the Doctor, and the other two Hector and the King of Egypt. "And now we've no Black Prince!" cried Robin, in dismay.

"Let Darkie be the Black Prince," said Nicholas. "When you have your stick he'll jump for it, and then you can pretend to fight with him."

"It's not a stick, it's a sword," said Robin "However, Darkie may be the Black Prince."

"And what's Pax to be?" asked Dora; "for you know he will come if Darkie does, and he'll run in before everybody else, too."

"Then he must be the Fool," said Robin; "and it will do very well, for the Fool comes in before the rest, and Pax can have his red coat on, and the collar with the little bells."

VI.

Robin thought that Christmas would never come. To the Captain and his wife it seemed to come too fast. They had hoped it might bring reconciliation with the old man, but it seemed they had hoped in vain.

There were times, now, when the Captain almost regretted the old bachelor's bequest. The familiar scenes of her old home sharpened his wife's grief. To see her father every Sunday in church, with marks of age and infirmity upon him, but with not a look of tenderness for his only child, this tried her sorely.

"She felt it less abroad," thought the Captain. "An English home, in which she frets herself to death, is, after all, no great boon."

Christmas Eve came.

"I'm sure it's quite Christmas enough, now," said Robin. "We'll have 'The Peace Egg' to-night."

So, as the Captain and his wife sat sadly over their fire, the door opened, and Pax ran in, shaking his bells, and followed by the nursery mummers. The performance was most successful. It was by no means pathetic, and yet, as has been said, the Captain's wife shed tears.

"What is the matter, mamma?" said St. George, abruptly dropping his sword and running up to her.

"Don't tease mamma with questions," said the Captain; "she is not very well, and rather sad. We must all be very kind and good to poor, dear mamma;" and the Captain raised his wife's hand to his lips as he spoke. Robin seized the other hand and kissed it tenderly. He was very fond of his mother. At this moment Pax took a little run and jumped on to mamma's lap, where, sitting facing the company, he opened his black mouth and yawned with a ludicrous inappropriateness worthy of any clown. It made everybody laugh.

"And now we'll go and act in the kitchen," said Nicholas.

"Supper at nine o'clock, remember," shouted the Captain. "And we are going to have real frumenty and Yule-cakes, such as mamma used to tell us of when we were abroad."

"Hurray!" shouted the mummers, and they ran off, Pax leaping from his seat just in time to hustle the Black Prince in the doorway.

When the dining-room door was shut, St. George raised his hand, and said, "Hush!"

The mummers pricked their ears, but there was only a distant harsh and scraping sound, as of stones rubbed together.

"They're cleaning the passages," St. George went on; "and Sarah told me they meant to finish the mistletoe, and have everything cleaned up by supper-time. They don't want us, I know. Look here; we will go real mumming, instead. That will be fun!"

The Valiant Slasher grinned with delight.

"But will mamma let us?" he inquired.

"Oh, it will be all right if we are back by supper-time," said St. George, hastily. "Only, of course, we must take care not to catch cold. Come and help me to get some wraps."

The old oak chest in which spare shawls, rugs, and coats were kept was soon ransacked, and the mummers' gay dresses hidden by motley wrappers. But no sooner did Darkie and Pax behold the coats, etc., than they at once began to leap and bark, as it was their custom to do when they saw any one dressing to go out.

Robin was sorely afraid that this would betray them; but, though the Captain and his wife heard the barking, they did not guess the cause. So, the front door being very gently opened and closed, the nursery mummers stole away.

VII.

It was a very fine night. The snow was well trodden on the drive, so that it did not wet their feet, but on the trees and shrubs it hung soft and white.

"It's much jollier being out at night than in the daytime," said Robin.

"Much," responded Nicholas, with intense feeling.

"We'll go a wassailing next week," said Robin. "I know all about it; and perhaps we shall get a good lot of money, and then we'll buy tin swords with scabbards for next year. I don't like these sticks. Oh, dear, I wish it wasn't so long between one Christmas and another."

"Where shall we go first?" asked Nicholas, as they turned into the high-road. But before Robin could reply, Dora clung to Nicholas, crying, "Oh, look at those men!"

The boys looked up the road, down which three men were coming in a very unsteady fashion, and shouting as they rolled from side to side.

"They're drunk," said Nicholas; "and they're shouting at us."

"Oh, run, run!" cried Dora; and down the road they ran, the men shouting and following them. They had not run far, when Hector caught his foot in the Captain's great-coat which he was wearing, and came down headlong in the road. They were close by a gate, and when Nicholas had set Hector on his legs, St. George hastily opened it.

"This is the first house," he said. "We'll act here;" and all, even the Valiant Slasher, pressed in as quickly as possible. Once safe within the grounds, they shouldered their sticks and resumed their composure.

"You're going to the front door," said Nicholas. "Mummers ought to go to the back."

"We don't know where it is," said Robin, and he rang the front-door bell. There was a pause. Then lights shone, steps were heard, and at last a sound of much unbarring, unbolting, and unlocking. It might have been a prison. Then the door was opened by an elderly, timid-looking woman, who held a tallow candle above her head.

"Who's there," she said, "at this time of night?"

"We're Christmas mummers," said Robin, stoutly; "we didn't know the way to the back door, but——"

"And don't you know better than to come here?" said the woman. "Be off with you, as fast as you can!"

"You're only the servant," said Robin. "Go and ask your master and mistress if they wouldn't like to see us act. We do it very well."

"You impudent boy, be off with you!" repeated the woman. "Master'd no more let you nor any other such rubbish set foot in this house——"

"Woman!" shouted a voice close behind her, which made her start as if she had been shot, "who authorizes you to say what your master will or will not do, before you ask him? The boy is right. You are the servant, and it is not your business to choose for me whom I shall or shall not see."

"I meant no harm, sir, I'm sure," said the house-keeper; "but I thought you'd never——"

"My good woman," said her master, "if I had wanted somebody to think for me, you're the last person I should have employed. I hire you to obey orders, not to think."

"I'm sure, sir," said the house-keeper, whose only form of argument was reiteration, "I never thought you would have seen them——"

"Then you were wrong," shouted her master. "I will see them. Bring them in."

He was a tall, gaunt old man, and Robin stared at him for some minutes, wondering where he could have seen somebody very like him. At last he remembered. It was the old gentleman of the blue cloak.

The children threw off their wraps, the house-keeper helping them, and chatting ceaselessly, from sheer nervousness.

"Well, to be sure," said she, "their dresses are pretty, too, and they seem quite a better sort of children; they talk quite genteel. I might ha' knowed they weren't like common mummers, but I was so flustered hearing the bell go so late, and——"

"Are they ready?" said the old man, who had stood like a ghost in the dim light of the flaring tallow candle, grimly watching the proceedings.

"Yes, sir. Shall I take them to the kitchen sir——"

"For you and the other idle hussies to gape and grin at? No. Bring them to the library," he snapped, and then he stalked off, leading the way.

The house-keeper accordingly led them to the library and then withdrew, nearly falling on her face as she left the room by stumbling over Darkie, who clipped in last like a black shadow.

The old man was seated in a carved oak chair by the fire.

"I never said the dogs were to come in," he said.

"But we can't do without them, please," said Robin, boldly. "You see, there are eight people in 'The Peace Egg,' and there are only five of us; and so Darkie has to be the Black Prince, and Pax has to be the Fool, and so we have to have them."

"Five and two make seven," said the old man, with a grim smile; "what do you do for the eighth?"

"Oh, that's the little one at the end," said Robin, confidentially. "Mamma said we weren't to mention him, but I think that's because we're children. You're grown up, you know, so I'll show you the book, and you can see for yourself," he went on, drawing "The Peace Egg" from his pocket. "There, that's the picture of him on the last page; black, with horns and a tail."

The old man's stern face relaxed into a broad smile as he examined the grotesque wood-cut; but, when he turned to the first page, the smile vanished in a deep frown, and his eyes shone like hot coals, with anger. He had seen Robin's name.

"Who sent you here?" he asked, in a hoarse voice. "Speak, and speak the truth! Did your mother send you here?"

Robin thought the old man was angry with them for playing truant. He said slowly, "N—no. She didn't exactly send us; but I don't think she'll mind our having come if we get back in time for supper. Mamma never forbid our going mumming, you know."

"I don't suppose she ever thought of it," Nicholas said, candidly, wagging his curly head from side to side.

"She knows we're mummers," said Robin, "for she helped us. When we were abroad, you know, she used to tell us about the mummers acting at Christmas when she was a little girl. And so we acted to papa and mamma, and so we thought we'd act to the maids, but they were cleaning the passages, and so we thought we'd really go mumming; and we've got several other houses to go to before supper-time. We'd better begin, I think," said Robin, and without more ado he began to march round and round, raising his sword and shouting,—

"I am St. George, who from Old England sprung,My famous name throughout the world hath rung."

And the performance went off quite as creditably as before.

As the children acted, the old man's anger wore off. He watched them with an interest he could not repress. When Nicholas took some hard thwacks from St. George without flinching, the old man clapped his hands; and, after the encounter between St. George and the Black Prince, he said he would not have the dogs excluded on any consideration. It was just at the end, when they were all marching round and round, holding on by each other's swords "over the shoulder," and singing "A mumming we will go, etc.," that Nicholas suddenly brought the circle to a stand-still by stopping dead short and staring up at the wall before him.

"What are you stopping for?" said St. George, turning indignantly round.

"Look there!" cried Nicholas, pointing to a little painting which hung above the old man's head.

Robin looked, and said, abruptly, "It's Dora."

"Which is Dora?" asked the old man, in a strange, sharp tone.

"Here she is," said Robin and Nicholas in one breath, as they dragged her forward.

"She's the Doctor," said Robin; "and you can't see her face for her things. Dor, take off your cap and pull back that hood. There! Oh, it is like her!"

It was a portrait of her mother as a child; but of this the nursery mummers knew nothing.

The old man looked as the peaked cap and hood fell away from Dora's face and fair curls and then he uttered a sharp cry and buried his head upon his hands. The boys stood stupefied, but Dora ran up to him and, putting her little hands on his arms, said, in childish, pitying tones, "Oh, I am so sorry! Have you got a headache? May Robin put the shovel in the fire for you? Mamma has hot shovels for her headaches." And, though the old man did not speak or move, she went on coaxing him and stroking his head, on which the hair was white. At this moment Pax took one of his unexpected runs and jumped on the old man's knee, in his own particular fashion, and then yawned at the company. The old man was startled, and lifted his face suddenly.

It was wet with tears.

"Why, you're crying!" exclaimed the children, with one breath.

"It's very odd," said Robin, fretfully. "I can't think what's the matter to-night. Mamma was crying, too, when we were acting; and papa said we weren't to tease her with questions; and he kissed her hand, and I kissed her hand, too. And papa said we must all be very kind to poor, dear mamma; and so I mean to be, she's so good. And I think we'd better go home, or perhaps she'll be frightened," Robin added.

"She's so good, is she?" asked the old man. He had put Pax off his knee and taken Dora on to it.

"Oh, isn't she!" said Nicholas, swaying his curly head from side to side as usual.

"She's always good," said Robin, emphatically; "and so's papa. But I'm always doing something I oughtn't to," he added, slowly. "But then you know I don't pretend to obey Sarah. I don't care a fig for Sarah; and I won't obey any woman but mamma."

"Who's Sarah?" asked the grandfather.

"She's our nurse," said Robin; "and she tells—I mustn't say what she tells,—but it's not the truth. She told one about you the other day," he added.

"About me?" said the old man.

"She said you were our grandpapa. So then I knew she was telling 'you know what.'"

"How did you know it wasn't true?" the old man asked.

"Why, of course," said Robin, "if you were our mamma's father, you'd know her, and be fond of her, and come and see her. And then you'd be our grandfather, too, and you'd have us to see you, and perhaps give us Christmas-boxes. I wish you were," Robin added, with a sigh; "it would be very nice."

"Would you like it?" asked the old man of Dora.

And Dora, who was half asleep and very comfortable, put her little arms about his neck as she was wont to put them round the Captain's, and said, "Very much."

He put her down at last, very tenderly, almost unwillingly, and left the children alone. By-and-by he returned, dressed in the blue cloak, and took Dora up again.

"I will see you home," he said.

The children had not been missed. The clock had only just struck nine when there came a knock on the door of the dining-room, where the Captain and his wife sat still by the Yule-log. She said "Come in," wearily, thinking it was the frumenty and the Christmas cakes.

But it was her father, with her child in his arms!

VIII.

Lucy Jane Bull and her sisters were quite old enough to understand a good deal of grownup conversation when they overheard it. Thus, when a friend of Mrs. Bull's observed, during an afternoon call, that she believed that "officers wives were very dressy," the young ladies were at once resolved to keep a sharp lookout for the Captain's wife's bonnet in church on Christmas day.

The Bulls had just taken their seats when the Captain's wife came in. They really would have hid their faces, and looked at the bonnet afterwards, but for the startling sight that met the gaze of the congregation. The old grandfather walked into the church abreast of the Captain.

"They've met in the porch," whispered Mr. Bull, under the shelter of his hat.

"They can't quarrel publicly in a place of worship," said Mrs. Bull, turning pale.

"She's gone into his seat," cried Lucy Jane, in a shrill whisper.

"And the children after her," added the other sister, incautiously aloud.

There was no doubt about the matter. The old man, in his blue cloak, stood for a few moments politely disputing the question of precedence with his handsome son-in-law. Then the Captain bowed and passed in, and the old man followed him.

By the time that the service was ended everybody knew of the happy peace-making, and was glad. One old friend after another came up with blessings and good wishes. This was a proper Christmas, indeed, they said. There was a general rejoicing.

But only the grandfather and his children knew that it was hatched from "The Peace Egg."

By a Bavarian Comrade.

"Over his tumbler of Gukguk he

sat reading journals, sometimes

contemplatively looking into

the clouds of his tobacco-pipe:

an agreeable phenomenon,—more

especially when he opened

his lips for speech."

Carlyle.

A STORY OF NUREMBERG.

It was a Christmas eve in the beginning of the sixteenth century, and through the streets of Nuremberg came drifting a feathery snow that heaped itself in fantastic patterns on the projecting windows and fretted stone balconies of the quaint and crowded houses. It was not an honest and single-minded snow-storm, such as would seek to shroud the whole city in its delicate white mantle, but rather a tricksy and capricious sprite, that neglected one spot to hurl itself with wanton violence on another. Borne on the breath of a keen and shifting wind, it came tossing gleefully full in the face of a solitary artisan who, wrapped in a heavy cloak, was making the best of his way homeward. Truly it was not a pleasant night to be abroad, with the snow-drifts dancing in your eyes like a million of tiny arrow-points, and the sharp wind cutting like a knife; and the wayfarer was consoling himself for his present discomfort by picturing the warm fireside and the hot supper that awaited him at home, when his cheerful dreams were broken by a sharp cry that seemed to come from under his very feet.

Startled, and not a little alarmed, he checked his rapid walk and listened. There was no mistaking the sound: it was neither imp nor fairy, but a real child, from whose little lungs came forth that wail at once pitiful and querulous. As he heard it, Peter Burkgmäier's kindly heart flew with one rapid bound to the cradle at home where slumbered his own infant daughter, and, hastily lowering his lantern, he searched under the dark archway whence the cry had come. There, sheltered by the wall and wrapped in a ragged cloak, was a baby boy, perhaps between two and three years old, but so tiny and emaciated as to seem hardly half that age. When the lantern flickered in his face he gave a frightened sob, and then lay quiet and exhausted in the strong arms that held him.

"Poor little wretch!" said the man. "Abandoned on Christmas eve to die in the snow!" And wrapping the child more closely in his own mantle, he hurried on until he reached his home, from whose latticed panes shone forth a cheerful stream of light. His wife, with her baby on her breast, met him at the door, and stared with a not unnatural amazement as her husband unrolled his cloak and showed her the boy, who, blinking painfully at the sudden light, tried to struggle down from his arms.

"See, Lisbeth!" he said, "I have found you a Christmas present where I least expected one—an unhappy baby left in the streets to die of cold and hunger."

His wife laid her own infant in the cradle and gazed alternately at her husband and at the child he carried. She was at all times slow to receive impressions, and slower yet to put her thoughts into words. When she spoke, it was without apparent emotion of any kind. "What are you going to do with him, Peter?" she said.

"What am I going to do with him?" was the reply. "I am going to feed and clothe and shelter him, and make an honest man out of him, please God. It cannot be that you would refuse the poor child a home?"

Lisbeth made no answer. She was a large, fair, sleepy-eyed woman, who had been accounted a beauty in her day. A model wife, too, people said; neat in dress, quiet of tongue, her conduct staid, her whole thoughts centred in her household. She now took the boy, noting with a woman's eye his coarse and ragged clothing, and stood him on his unsteady little feet. A faint expression of disgust rippled over her smooth, unthinking face.

"He is a humpback," she said, slowly.

Her husband started to his feet. In all ages physical deformity has been a thing repulsive to our eyes; but at this early day it was regarded with unmixed horror and aversion, and was too often considered as the index of a crooked mind within. Peter Burkgmäier, tall and erect, with a frame of iron and sinews of steel, as became a master stone-mason, stood gazing at the poor little atom of misshapen humanity who tottered over the polished wooden floor. The spinal column was sadly bent, and from between the humped shoulders the pale face peered with an old, uncanny look. Yet the boy was not otherwise ugly. His forehead was broad and smooth, and his dark blue eyes were well and deeply set. The artisan watched him for a minute in painful silence, then turned to his wife and took her passive hand in his.

"Lisbeth," he said, with grave kindness, "I know that I am asking a great deal of you when I beg you to take this child under our roof. He will be to you much care and trouble, and may never find his way into your heart. At any other time, believe me, I would not put this burden on your shoulders. But it is Christmas eve, and were I to refuse a shelter to this helpless baby I would feel like one of those who had no room within their inns for the Holy Child. Dear wife, will you not receive him for love of me and of God, and let him share with little Kala in your care?"

Lisbeth's only reply was one characteristic of the woman. She was moved by her husband's appeal, against what she considered her better judgment; and without a single word she picked up the boy from the floor and laid him in the cradle by the side of her own little daughter. Then, with a smile—and her smiles came but rarely—she proceeded to carry off Peter's wet cloak and to bring in his supper. So with this mute assent the matter was settled, and the deformed child was received into the stone-mason's family.

And in a different way he became the source of much gratification to both husband and wife. The first regarded him with real kindness and an almost fatherly affection, for the boy soon began to manifest a quick intelligence and a winning gentleness that might readily have found their way into a harder heart. Lisbeth, too, had her reward; for it was sweet to her soul to hear her neighbors say, as they stopped to watch the two children playing in the doorway: "Ah! Lisbeth, it is not many a woman who would take the care you do of a wretched little humpback like that;" or, "It was a lucky chance for the poor child that threw him into such hands as yours, Mistress Burkgmäier;" or, "Did ever little Kala look so fair and straight as when she had that crooked boy by her side?"

And did not the good pastor from the Frauenkirche say to her, with tears starting in his gentle eyes: "God will surely reward you for your kindness to this helpless little one?" Nay, better yet, did not the Stadtholder's lady lean out from her beautiful carriage, and say before three of the neighbors, who were standing by and heard every word: "You are a good woman, Mistress Burkgmäier, to take the same care of this miserable child as of your own pretty little daughter"?—which was something to be really proud of; for, whereas it was the obvious duty of a priest to admire a virtuous act, it was not often that a noble lady deigned thus to express her approbation.

Yes, Lisbeth felt, as she listened serenely to all this praise—surely so well merited—that there was some compensation in the world for such charitable deeds as hers, even when they involved a fair amount of sacrifice. And little Gabriel, before whom many of these remarks were uttered, pondered over them in secret, and gradually evolved three facts from the curious puzzle of his life—first, that he did not really belong to what seemed to be his home; second, that he was not loved in it as was Kala; third, that Kala was pretty and he was ugly. So with these three melancholy scraps of knowledge the poor child began his earthly education.

And Kala was very pretty. Tall and strong-limbed, with her mother's beautiful hair and skin, and with her mother's clear, meaningless blue eyes, the little girl attracted attention wherever she was seen. No better foil to her vigorous young beauty could have been found than the pale, misshapen boy whom all the world called ugly. The children played together under Lisbeth's watchful eye, and Gabriel in all things yielded to his companion's imperious will, so that peace reigned ever over their sports. But when Sigmund Wahnschaffe, the son of the bronze-worker in the neighboring street, joined them, then Kala would have no more of Gabriel's company. For Sigmund was strong as a young

Hercules and surpassed all the other lads in their boyish games. When he would play with her, Kala turned her back ungratefully upon the patient companion of her idler moments, who was fain to watch in silence the pleasures he might not share.

Yet from Sigmund she met no easy compliance with her wishes. His will was a law not to be disputed, and once, when she had ventured to assert herself in rebellious fashion, he promptly maintained his precedence by pushing her into the mud. Kala began to cry, and, like a flash, Gabriel, in a storm of rage, flung himself upon the older boy, only to be shaken off as a feather into the same muddy gutter. It was over in a minute, nor would Sigmund deign to further punish the little humpback who had been ridiculous enough to attack him. Serenely unmoved he strolled away, while Kala and Gabriel went sadly home together, to be both well scolded for the ruin of their clothes and sent supperless to bed; Lisbeth priding herself, above all things, on the strictly impartial character of her retributive justice.

But Gabriel had at least one pastime which could be shared with none, and which bade fair to recompense him for all the childish sports he was denied. With a small block of wood and a few simple tools his skilful fingers wrought such wonders that Kala and Sigmund, and the very children who hooted at him in the street, could not withhold their admiration,—sometimes a brooding dove with pretty, ruffled plumage; sometimes the head and curving horns of a mountain chamois, instinct with graceful life; sometimes a group of snails, each tiny spiral reproduced with loving accuracy in the hard grained wood. To Peter Burkgmäier these evidences of a talent then in such high repute gave most unbounded satisfaction. His own trade was far too severe for the boy's frail strength, but wood-carving was fully as profitable, and might lead to wealth and fame. Had not Veit Stoss, of whose genius Nuremberg felt justly proud, already finished his wonderful group of angels saluting the Virgin, which hung from the roof of St. Lorenz? With such an example before him, what might not the boy hope to achieve through talent and persevering labor? And Gabriel felt his own heart burn as he looked with wistful eyes upon that masterpiece of rare and delicate carving.

Nuremberg was then alive with the spirit of art, and everywhere he turned there was something beautiful to quicken his pulse and feed the flame within his soul, that was half rapture and half bitterness. No idle boast was the old rhyme,—

"Nuremberg's handGoes through every land."

For the city's renown had spread far and wide, and in its many branches of industry, as well as in the higher walks of art, it had reached the zenith of its fame. Already, indeed, the canker-worm was gnawing at the root, and unerring retribution was creeping on a blinded people; but no sign of the future was manifested in the universal prosperity of the day. Every street furnished its food for the artist's soul: the Frauenkirche, enriched with the loving gifts of devout generations; St. Sebald's, with its carved portal, its stained windows, its treasures of bronze, and, above all, the shrine where Peter Vischer and his sons labored for thirteen years. Gabriel loved St. Sebald's dearly, but closer still to his heart was the majestic church of St. Lorenz, where, in sharp relief against the dull red pillars, rose that dream in stone, the Sacrament House of

Adam Krafft, its slender, fretted spire springing to the very roof, clasped in the embrace of the curling vine tendrils carved around it.

Here the boy would linger for hours, never weary of studying every detail of this faultless shrine. With envious eyes he gazed upon the kneeling figures of Adam Krafft and his two fellow-laborers, who, carved in stone, now supported the treasure their hands had wrought. Surely this was the crowning summit of human ambition—to live thus forever in the house of God, and before the eyes of men, a part of the very work which had ennobled the artist's life. Ah! if he, the despised humpback, could but descend to posterity immortalized by the labor of his hands. What to the dreaming lad was the picture of Adam Krafft dying in a hospital, poor, unfriended, and alone, in the midst of a city his genius had enriched? What was it to him that Nuremberg, which now heaped honors on the dead, had denied bread to the living? Such bitter truths come not to the young. They are the heritage of age, and Gabriel was but a boy, with all a boy's fond hopes and aspirations. Often as he studied the graceful beauty of the Sacrament House, where, cut in the pure white stone, he saw the Last Supper and Christ blessing little children, he wondered whether among those Jewish boys and girls was one who, deformed and repulsive to the eye, yet felt the Saviour's loving touch and was comforted.

A few more years rolled by, and each succeeding spring saw Kala taller and prettier, and Gabriel working harder still at his laborious art. Not so engrossed, however, but that he knew that Kala was fair, and that when her soft fingers touched his a swift and sudden fire leaped through his heart. Kala's beauty lurked in his dreams by night and in his long, solitary days of toil, and became the motive power of all his best endeavors. If he should gain wealth, it would be but to lay it at her feet. If he, the desolate waif, should win fame and distinction, it would be but to gild her name with his. Surely these things must be some recompense in a woman's eyes for a pale face and a stunted form; and Gabriel, lost in foolish dreams, worked on.

Sigmund Wahnschaffe, too, had grown into early manhood and had adopted his father's calling. Strong arms were as useful in their way as a creative brain, and if Sigmund could never be an artist like Peter Vischer, he promised at least to make an excellent workman. People said he was the handsomest young artisan in Nuremberg, with his dark skin bronzed by the fires among which he labored, and his black eyes sparkling with a keen and merry light. Times had changed since the day he pushed little Kala into the mud, and he looked upon her now as some frail and delicate blossom, that to handle would be desecration. Yet Kala was no rare flower, but a common plant, with nothing remarkable about her except her beauty; and, once married, Sigmund would be prompt enough to recognize this fact. Gabriel, with a chivalrous and imaginative soul, might perhaps retain his ideal unbroken till his death; but in the young bronze-worker's practical mind ideals had no place, and his bride would slip naturally into the post of housewife, from whom nothing more exalted would be demanded than thrifty habits and a cheerful temper.

And Kala knew perfectly that both these young men loved her, and that one day she would be called upon to choose between them, between Sigmund, strong, handsome, and resolute, with a laugh and a gay word for all who met him; and Gabriel, dwarfed and silent, who had caught the trick of melancholy in his unloved childhood and could not shake it off. But it was not merely the sense of physical deformity that saddened Gabriel's soul. The air he breathed was filled with a subtle spirit of discord; for upon Nuremberg, with her many churches and monuments of mediæval art, the Reformation had laid its chilling hand. Its influence was felt on every side—in art, where the joyous simplicity of Wohlgemuth had given place to the fantastic melancholy of Albrecht Dürer, fit imprint of a troubled and storm-tossed mind; as well as in literature, where the bitter raillery and coarse jests of Hans Sachs, the cobbler-poet, now passed with swift approval from mouth to mouth.

The day had not yet come when Nuremberg, in her blind arrogance, was to close her gates upon those who had given her life and fame; but already were heard the first faint murmurs of the approaching storm. What wonder that Gabriel shrank from the darkening future, and that men like Peter Burkgmäier, pondering with set mouths and frowning brows, were slowly making up their minds that the city which had been their birthplace should never shelter their old age. But Lisbeth went stolidly about the daily routine of her life; Kala's smiles were as bright and as frequent as ever; and Sigmund troubled himself not at all with matters beyond his ken.

Winter had set in early, and already November had brought in its train snow and biting winds, and the promise of severe cold to come. It was a busy season for the bronze-workers, and Sigmund toiled unceasingly, his cheerful thoughts giving zest to his labors and new strength to his mighty arm. For did not each evening see him by Kala's side, and had she not, after months of vain coquetting, at last fairly yielded up her heart?

"Kala will make a good wife," said Lisbeth, proudly. "And she goes not empty-handed to her husband's house."

"They are a well-matched pair," said Peter, meditatively. "Health and beauty and dulness are no mean heritage in these troubled times."

And though the neighbors hesitated to call the young couple dull, they one and all agreed that the marriage was a suitable one, and that they had long foreseen it. "Why, they were little lovers in childhood, even!" said Theresa, the wife of Johann Dyne, the toy-vender in the next street; and Kala, who had perhaps forgotten the time when her child-lover had knocked her into the gutter, smiled, and showed her beautiful white teeth, and suffered the remark to pass uncontradicted.

But even the most stolid of women have always some lurking tenderness for those who they know have loved them vainly, and Kala, though she had without a demur accepted Sigmund for her husband, yet broke the news to Gabriel with much gentleness, and was greatly comforted by the apparent composure with which it was received. He grew perhaps a trifle paler and quieter than before, if such a thing were possible, and shut himself up more resolutely with his work; but that was all. No one would have dreamed that life with its fair promises had suddenly grown worthless in his hands, and that the rich gifts which still were left him seemed as nothing compared with the valueless treasure he had lost. Even his art had become hateful, freighted as it was with dead hopes; and often, when all believed him to be toiling in his little den, he was wandering aimlessly through the streets of Nuremberg, seeking comfort in those haunts which had once been to him as dear friends and companions. For hours he would linger in the church of St. Lorenz, and then slowly make his way to the Thiergarten Gate, where, along the Seilersgasse to the churchyard, rise at regular intervals the seven stone pillars on which Adam Krafft has carved, in beautiful bas-reliefs, scenes from the Passion of the Lord. Years before the simple piety of a Nuremberg citizen had erected these monuments of holy art, and their founder, Martin Ketzel, had even travelled into Palestine, that he might measure the exact distances of that most sorrowful journey from the house of Pontius Pilate to the hill of Calvary. Heedless of the severe weather, Gabriel visited daily these primitive stations, striving to forget his own bitterness in the presence of a divine grief; and, laying his troubled heart at his Saviour's feet, would return, strengthened and comforted, into the busy city.

Christmas now was drawing near, and with its approach a new resolve took possession of his soul. A fresh light had dawned upon him, and, shaking off his apathy, he started to work in earnest. All day long he toiled with a steady purpose, though none were permitted to see the fruit of his labors. Kala, indeed, unaccustomed to be thwarted in her curiosity, presented herself at his work-shop door and implored admittance; but not even to her was the secret revealed.

"It is very unkind of you!" she pouted, hardly doubting that she would gain her point. "You never kept anything from me in your life before."

Gabriel took her hand and looked with strange, wistful eyes into her pretty face. "I am keeping nothing from you now," he said. "It is your wedding-gift that I am fashioning; but you must be content to wait its completion before you see it. By Christmas it shall be your own."

So Kala, comforted with the thought of future possession, bided her time, and Gabriel was left in undisputed enjoyment of his solitude. At first he worked languidly and with little zest; but from interest grew ambition, and from ambition a passionate love for the labor of his hands, which threw all other hopes and fears into the background. Kala was forgotten, and Gabriel, absorbed in the contemplation of his art and striving as he had never striven before, felt as though some power not his own were working in him, and that the supreme effort of his life had come. Yet ever in the midst of his feverish activity a strange weakness seized and held him powerless in its grasp; and like a keen and sudden pain came the bitter thought that he might die before his work was done. Instinctively he felt that his hopes of future fame rested on these few weeks that were flying pitilessly by, each one carrying with it some portion of his wasted strength; and that if death should overtake him with his labor uncompleted his name and memory must perish from the world. So, like one who flies across a Russian steppe pursued by starving wolves, Gabriel sped on his task, seeking to out-distance the grim and noiseless wolf that followed close upon his track.

It was Christmas eve, the anniversary of that snowy night when Peter Burkgmäier had carried home the deformed child, and now all was bustle and glad preparation in the stone-mason's household. Within three days Kala was to be married, and Lisbeth, who felt that her reputation as cook and housewife was at stake, spared neither time nor trouble in her hospitable labors. Since early morning the great fires had roared in her spacious kitchen, and all the poor who came to beg a Christmas bounty tasted freely of her good cheer. With light heart and busy fingers Kala assisted her mother, and doled out the bread and cakes—not too lavishly—to the ragged children who clamored around the door; wondering much in the meanwhile what trinket Sigmund would bring her with which to deck herself on Christmas morning.

And in his little room Gabriel stood looking at his finished work, and asking himself if his heart spoke truly when it whispered: "You, too, are great." It was sweet to realize that his task was done and that he might rest at last; it was sweeter still to see in the bit of carved wood before him the fulfilment of all his dearest dreams. So, while daylight faded into dusk and evening into night, he sat lost in a maze of tangled thoughts that crowded wearily through his listless brain. It was now too dark for him to discern the image by his side, but from time to time he laid his hand upon it with a gentle touch, as a mother might caress a sleeping child, and was happy in its dumb companionship.

How long he had been sitting thus he never knew, when suddenly out into the frosty air rang the great bells of St. Lorenz, calling the faithful to midnight Mass.

Clearly and joyfully they pealed, as if their brazen tongues were striving to utter in words their messages of good-will to men. Gabriel's heart leaped at the sound, and a great yearning seized him to kneel once more within those beloved walls, and amid their solemn beauty to adore the new-born Babe. Jubilantly rang the bells, and their glad voices seemed to speak to him as old friends, and with one accord to urge him on. Weak and dizzy, he crept down the narrow stairs and out into the bitter night. The sharp wind struck him in the face, and worried him as it had worried years before the baby abandoned to its cruel embraces. Yet with the appealing music of the bells ringing in his ears he never thought of turning back, but struggled bravely onward until the frowning walls of St. Lorenz rose up before him. Through the open doors poured a little crowd of devotees, and Gabriel, entering, stole softly up to the Sacrament House, where so often the carved Christ had looked with gentle eyes upon his lonely childhood.

Mass had begun, and the great church was hardly a third full, for Nuremberg's weakening faith exempted her children from such untimely services. But in the faces of the scattered worshippers there was something never seen before—a grave severity, a solemn purpose, as when men are banded together to resist in silence an advancing foe. Gabriel, dimly conscious of this, strove to restrain his wandering thoughts, and fixed his eyes upon the gleaming altar. But no prayer rose to his lips, though into his heart came that deep sense of rest and contentment which found an utterance long ago in the words of an apostle: "Lord, it is good for us to be here." Like a child he had come to his Father's feet, and, laying there his rejected human love, his ungratified human ambition, he gained in their place the peace which passeth all understanding. The two shadows which had mocked him during life vanished into nothingness at the hour of death, and with clear eyes he saw the value of an immortal soul.

Mass was over, and the congregation moved slowly through the shadowy aisles out into the starlit night. But Gabriel sat still, his head resting against the stone pillar, his dead eyes fixed upon the Sacrament House, and upon the sculptured Christ rising triumphant from the grave.

Four weeks had gone by since the body of the humpback had been carried sorrowfully past the stations of the Seilersgasse into the quiet churchyard beyond. The dusk of a winter evening shrouded the empty streets when a stranger, of grave demeanor and in the prime of life, knocked at the stone-mason's door. Kala opened it, and her father, recognizing the visitor, rose with wondering respect to greet him. It was Veit Stoss, the wood-carver, then at the zenith of his fame. With quick, keen eyes he glanced around the homely room, taking in every detail of the scene before him—Lisbeth weaving placidly by the fire; Kala fair and blushing in the lamp-light; and Sigmund playing idly with the crooked little turnspit at his feet. Then he turned to Peter, and for a minute the two men stood looking furtively at one another, as though each were trying to read his companion's thoughts. Finally, the wood-carver spoke.

"I grieve, Master Burkgmäier," he said, with courteous sympathy, "that you should have lost your foster-son, to whom report says you were much attached. And I hear also that the young man promised highly in his calling."

"Then you heard not all," answered the stone-mason, slowly. "Gabriel did more, for he fulfilled his promise."

A sudden light came into the artist's eyes. "It is true, then," he said, eagerly, "that the boy left behind him a rare piece of work, which has not yet been seen outside these walls. I heard the rumor, but thought it idle folly."

Peter Burkgmäier crossed the room and opened a deep cupboard. "You shall see it," he said simply, "and answer for yourself. No one in Nuremberg is more fit to judge." Then, lifting out something wrapped in a heavy cloth, he carried it to the table, unveiled it with a reverent hand, and, stepping back, waited in silence for a verdict.

There was a long, breathless pause, broken only by the low whir of Lisbeth's busy wheel. Veit Stoss stood motionless, while Peter's eyes never stirred from the table before them. There, carved in the fair white wood, rested the divine Babe, as on that blessed Christmas night when his Mother "wrapped him up in swaddling-clothes and laid him in a manger." The lovely little head nestled on its rough pillow as though on Mary's bosom; the tiny limbs were relaxed in sleep; the whole figure breathed at once the dignity of the Godhead and the pathetic helplessness of babyhood. Instinctively one loved, and pitied, and adored. Nor was this all. Every broken bit of straw that thrust its graceful, fuzzy head from between the rough bars of the manger, every twisted knot of grass, every gnarl and break in the wood itself, had been wrought with the tender accuracy of the true artist, who finds nothing too simple for his utmost care and skill.

Veit Stoss drew a heavy breath and turned to his companion. "It is a masterpiece," he said, gravely, "which I should be proud to call my own. I congratulate you on the possession of so great a treasure."

"It is not mine," returned the artisan, "but my daughter's. Gabriel wrought it for her wedding-gift."

The wood-carver's keen blue eyes scanned Kala's pretty, stolid face, and then wandered to Sigmund's broad shoulders and mighty bulk. A faint, derisive smile curled his well-cut lips. "Your daughter's beauty merits, indeed, the rarest of all rare tokens," he said, slowly. "But perhaps there are other things more needful to a young housewife than even this precious bit of carving. If she will part with it I will pay her seventy thalers, and it shall lie in St. Sebald's Church near my own Virgin, that all may see its loveliness and remember the hand that fashioned it."

Seventy thalers! Sigmund dropped the dog and lifted his handsome head with a look of blank bewilderment. Seventy thalers for a bit of wood like that, when his own strong arms could not earn as much in months! He stared at the little image in wondering perplexity, as though striving to see by what mysterious process it had arrived at such a value; while into his heart crept a thought strictly in keeping with his practical nature. If the humpback could have produced work worth so much, what a thousand pities he should die with only one piece finished!

On Lisbeth, too, a revelation seemed to have fallen. Her wheel had stopped, and in her mind she was rapidly running over a list of household goods valued at seventy thalers. It was a mental calculation quickly and cleverly accomplished; for Lisbeth was not slow in all things, and years of thrift had taught her the full worth of money. Instinctively she glanced at her husband and marvelled at his unmoved face.

"Your offer is a liberal one, Master Stoss," said Peter, gravely. "And I rejoice to think that the poor lad's genius will be recognized. In him Nuremberg would have had another famous son."

"In him Nuremberg has now a famous son," corrected Veit Stoss, laying his hand upon the statue. "No other proof of greatness can be needed." With gentle care he replaced the cloth and lifted the precious burden in his arms, when suddenly Kala sprang forward, her cheeks ablaze, her blue eyes dark with anger. Transfigured for one instant into a new and passionate beauty, she snatched the image from his hands.

"It is mine!" she cried, fiercely; "mine! Gabriel loved me, and carved it for me when he knew that he was dying. It was for me he did it, and you shall not take it from me."

She gathered it to her bosom with a low, broken cry, and darted from the room. God only knows what late love, and pity, and remorse were working in her breast. Veit Stoss turned softly to her father. "It is enough," he said. "Your daughter has the prior right, and I came not here to wrong her."

And so the hand which had robbed Gabriel of love and life robbed him of fame. For the statue which should have given joy to generations remained unknown in the artisan's family. At first many came to see and wonder at its beauty; but with the advent of a colder creed men wanted not such tokens of a vanished fervor, and the little Christ-Child was soon forgotten by the world. Perhaps Kala's sturdy grandchildren destroyed it as a useless toy; perhaps it perished by fire, or flood, or evil accident. No memory of it lingers in the streets of Nuremberg; and Gabriel, lifted beyond the everlasting hills, knoweth the vanity of all human wishes.

The Italian Guest's Selection.

"He is a Tuscan born, of an old

noble race in that part of Italy."

Hawthorne.

A PICTURE OF THE NATIVITY BY FRA FILIPPO LIPPI

as explained by a pious florentine gossip of his day.

"Now, I cannot affirm that things did really take place in this manner, but it greatly pleases me to think that they did."—Fra Domenico Cavalca: *Life of the Magdalen*.

The silly folks do not at all understand about the birth of our Lord. They say that our Lord was born at Bethlehem, and because the inns were all full, owing to certain feasts kept by those Jews, in a stable. But I tell you this is an error, and due to little sense, for our Lord was indeed placed in a manger, because none of the hostleries would receive Joseph and the Blessed Virgin; but it took place differently.

For you must know that beyond Bethlehem, which is a big village walled and moated, of those parts, lies a hilly country, exceeding wild, and covered with dense woods of firs, pines, larches, beeches, and similar trees, which the people of Bethlehem cut down at times, going in bands, and burn to charcoal, packing it on mules, to sell in the valley; or tie together whole trunks such as serve for beams, rafters, and masts, and float them down the rivers, which are many and very rapid.

In these mountains, then, in the thickest part of the woods, a certain man, of the wood-cutting trade, bethought him to build a house wherein to store the timber and live, himself and his family, when so it pleased him, and keep his beasts; and for this purpose he employed certain pillars and pieces of masonry that stood in the forest, being remains of a temple of the heathen, the which had long ceased to exist. And he cleared the wood round about, leaving only tree stumps and bushes; and close by in a ravine, between high fir-trees, ran a river, always full to the brim even in midsummer, owing to the melting snows, and of greenish waters, cold and rapid exceedingly; and around, up hill and down dale, stretched the wood of firs, larches, pines, and other noble and useful trees, emitting a very pleasant and virtuous fragrance. The man thought to enjoy his house, and came with his family, and servants, and horses, and mules, and oxen, which he had employed to carry down the timber and charcoal.

A Hilly country

But scarcely were they settled than an earthquake rent the place, tearing wall from wall and pillar from pillar, and a voice was heard in the air, crying, "Ecce domus domini dei." Whereupon they fled, astonished and in terror, and returned into the town.

And no one of that man's family ventured henceforth to return to that wood, or to that house, save one called Hilarion, a poor lad and a servant, but of upright heart and faith in the Lord, which offered to go back and take his abode there, and cut down the trees and burn the charcoal for his master.

So he went, being a poor lad and poorly clad in leathern tunic and coarse serge hood. And Hilarion took with him an ox and an ass to load with charcoal and drive down to Bethlehem to his master.

And the first night that Hilarion slept in that house, which was fallen to ruin, only a piece of roof remaining, which he thatched with pine-branches, he heard voices singing in the air, as of children, both boys and maidens. But he closed his eyes and repeated a Paternoster, and turned over and slept. And again, another night, he heard voices, and knew the house to be haunted, and trembled. But, being clear of heart, he said two Aves and went to sleep. And once more did he hear voices, and they were passing sweet; and with them came a fragrance as of crushed herbs, and many kinds of flowers, and frankincense, and orris-root; and Hilarion shook, for he feared lest it be the heathen gods, Mercury, or Macomet, or Apollinis. But he said his prayer and slept.

But at length, one night, as Hilarion heard those songs as usual, he opened his eyes. And, behold! the place was light, and a great staircase of light, like golden cobwebs, stretched up to heaven, and there were angels going about in numbers, coming and going, with locks like honeycomb, and dresses pink, and green, and sky-blue, and white, thickly embroidered with purest pearls, and wings as of butterflies and peacock's tails, with glories of solid gold about their head. And they went to and fro, carrying garlands and strewing flowers, so that, although mid-winter, it was like a garden in June, so sweet of roses, and lilies, and gillyflowers. And the angels sang; and when they had finished their work, they said, "It is well," and departed, holding hands and flying into the sky above the fir-trees.

And Hilarion wondered greatly, and said five Paters and six Aves. And the next day, as he was cutting a fir-tree in the wood, there met him, among the rocks, a man old, venerable, with a long gray beard and a solemn air. And he was clad in crimson, and under his arm he carried written books and a scourge. And Hilarion said,—

"Who art thou? for this forest is haunted by spirits, and I would know whether thou be of them or of men."

And the ancient made answer: "My name is Hieronymus. I am a wise man and a king. I have spent all my days learning the secrets of things. I know how the trees grow and waters run, and where treasure lies; and I can teach thee what the stars sing, and in what manner the ruby and emerald are smelted in the bowels of the earth; and I can chain the winds and stop the sun, for I am wise above all men. But I seek one wiser than myself, and go through the woods in search of him, my master."

169

And Hilarion said: "Tarry thou here, and thou shalt see, if I mistake not, him whom thou seekest."

So the old man, whose name was Hieronymus, tarried in the forest and built himself a hut of stones.

And the day after that, as Hilarion went forth to catch fish in the river, he met on the bank a lady, beautiful beyond compare, the which for all clothing wore only her own hair, golden and exceeding long. And Hilarion asked,—

"Who art thou? for this forest is haunted by spirits, and I would know whether thou art one of such, and of evil intent, as the demon Venus, or a woman like the mother who bore me."

And the lady answered: "My name is Magdalen. I am a princess and a courtesan, and the fairest woman that ever be. All day the princes and kings of the earth have brought gifts to my house, and hung wreaths on my roof, and strewed flowers in my yard; and the poets all day have sung to their lutes, and all have lain groaning at my gates at night; for I am beautiful beyond all creatures. But I seek one more beautiful than myself, and go searching my master by the lakes and the rivers."

And Hilarion made answer: "Tarry thou here, and thou shalt see, if I mistake not, him whom thou seekest?"

And the lady, whose name was Magdalen, tarried by the river and built herself a cabin of reeds and leaves. And that night was the longest and coldest of the winter.

And Hilarion made for himself a bed of fern and hay in the stable of the ox and the ass, and lay close to them for warmth. And, lo! in the middle of the night the ass brayed and the ox bellowed, and Hilarion started up.

And he saw the heavens open with a great brightness as of beaten and fretted gold, and angels coming and going, and holding each other by the hand, and wreathed in roses, and singing "Gloria in Excelsis Deo, et in terra pax hominibus bonæ voluntatis."

And Hilarion wondered and said ten Paters and ten Aves.

And that day, towards noon, there came through the wood one bearing a staff, and leading a mule, on which was seated a woman, that was near unto her hour and moaning piteously. And they were poor folk and travel-stained.

And the man said to Hilarion: "My name is Joseph. I am a carpenter from the city of Nazareth, and my wife is called Mary, and she is in travail. Suffer thou us to rest, and my wife to lie on the straw of the stable."

And Hilarion said: "You are welcome. Benedictus qui venit in nomine domini;" and Hilarion laid down more fern and hay, and gave provender to the mule. And the woman's hour came, and she was delivered of a male child. And Hilarion took it and laid it in the manger. And he went forth into the woods and found the ancient wizard Hieronymus, and the lady Magdalen, and said,—

"Come with me to the ruined house, for truly there is He whom you be seeking."

And they followed him to the ruined house where the fir-trees were cleared above the river; and they saw the babe lying in the manger, and Hieronymus and Magdalen kneeled down, saying, "Surely this is He that is our Master, for He is wiser and more fair than either."

And the skies opened, and there came forth angels, such as Hilarion had seen, with glories of solid gold round their heads, and garlands of roses about their necks, and they took hands and danced, and sang, flying up, "Gloria in Excelsis Deo."

By The Stay-At-Home Traveller.

"He prepares to read by wiping

his spectacles, carefully adjusting

them on his eyes, and drawing

the candle close to him—is

very particular in having his

slippers ready for him at the

fire."

Hunt.

MELCHIOR'S DREAM.

"Well, father, I don't believe the Browns are a bit better off than we are; and yet, when I spent the day with young Brown, we cooked all sorts of messes in the afternoon; and he wasted twice as much rum and brandy and lemons in his trash as I should want to make good punch of. He was quite surprised, too, when I told him that our mince-pies were kept shut up in the larder, and only brought out at meal-times, and then just one apiece; he said they had mince-pies always going, and he got one whenever he liked. Old Brown never blows up about that sort of thing; he likes Adolphus to enjoy himself in the holidays, particularly at Christmas."

The speaker was a boy—if I may be allowed to use the word in speaking of an individual whose jackets had for some time past been resigned to a younger member of his family, and who daily, in the privacy of his own apartment, examined his soft cheeks by the aid of his sisters' "back-hair glass." He was a handsome boy, too; tall, and like David—"ruddy, and of a fair countenance;" and his face, though clouded then, bore the expression of general amiability. He was the eldest son in a large young family, and was being educated at one of the best public schools. He did not, it must be confessed, think either small beer or small beans of himself; and as to the beer and beans that his family thought of him, I think it was pale ale and kidney-beans at least.

When the lords of the creation of all ages can find nothing else to do, they generally take to eating and drinking; and so it came to pass that our hero had set his mind upon brewing a jorum of punch, and sipping it with an accompaniment of mince-pies; and Paterfamilias had not been quietly settled to his writing for half an hour, when he was disturbed by an application for the necessary ingredients. These he had refused, quietly explaining that he could not afford to waste his French brandy, etc., in school-boy cookery, and ending with, "You see the reason, my dear boy?"

To which the dear boy replied as above, and concluded with the disrespectful (not to say ungrateful) hint, "Old Brown never blows up about that sort of thing; he likes Adolphus to enjoy himself in the holidays."

Whereupon Paterfamilias made answer, in the mildly deprecating tone in which the elder sometimes do answer the younger in these topsy-turvy days:—

"That's quite a different case. Don't you see, my boy, that Adolphus Brown is an only son, and you have nine brothers and sisters? If you have punch and mince-meat to play with, there is no reason why Tom should not have it, and James, and Edward, and William, and Benjamin, and Jack. And then there are your sisters. Twice the amount of the Browns' mince-meat would not serve you. The Christmas bills, too, are very heavy, and I have a great many calls on my purse; and you must be reasonable. Don't you see?"

"Well, father——" began the boy; but his father interrupted him. He knew the unvarying beginning of a long grumble, and dreading the argument, cut it short.

"I have decided. You must amuse yourself some other way. And just remember that young Brown's is quite another case. He is an only son."

Whereupon Paterfamilias went off to his study and his sermon; and his son, like the Princess in Andersen's story of the swineherd, was left outside to sing,—

"O dearest Augustine, All's clean gone away!"

Not that he did say that—that was the princess's song—what he said was,—

"I wish I were an only son!"

This was rather a vain wish, for round the dining-room fire (where he soon joined them) were gathered his nine brothers and sisters, who, to say the truth, were not looking much more lively and cheerful than he. And yet (of all days in the year on which to be doleful and dissatisfied!) this was Christmas Eve.

Now I know that the idea of dulness or discomfort at Christmas is a very improper one, particularly in a story. We all know how every little boy in a story-book spends the Christmas holidays. First, there is the large hamper of good things sent by grandpapa, which is as inexhaustible as Fortunatus's purse, and contains everything, from a Norfolk turkey to grapes from the grandpaternal vinery. There is the friend who gives a guinea to each member of the family, and sees who will spend it best. There are the godpapas and godmammas, who might almost be fairy sponsors from the number of expensive gifts that they bring upon the scene. The uncles and aunts are also liberal.

One night is devoted to a magic-lantern (which has a perfect focus), another to the pantomime, a third to a celebrated conjurer, a fourth to a Christmas tree and juvenile ball.

The happy youth makes himself sufficiently ill with plum-pudding, to testify to the reader how good it was, and how much there was of it; but recovers in time to fall a victim to the negus and trifle at supper for the same reason. He is neither fatigued with late hours, nor surfeited with sweets; or if he is, we do not hear of it.

But as this is a strictly candid history, I will at once confess the truth, on behalf of my hero and his brothers and sisters. They had spent the morning in decorating the old church, in pricking holly about the house, and in making a mistletoe bush. Then in the afternoon they had tasted the Christmas soup, and seen it given out; they had put a finishing touch to the snowman by crowning him with holly, and had dragged the yule-logs home from the carpenter's. And now, the early tea being over, Paterfamilias had gone to finish his sermon for to-morrow; his friend was shut up in his room; and Materfamilias was in hers, with one of those painful headaches which even Christmas will not always keep away. So the ten children were left to amuse themselves, and they found it rather a difficult matter.

"Here's a nice Christmas!" said our hero. He had turned his youngest brother out of the arm-chair, and was now lying in it with his legs over the side. "Here's a nice Christmas! A fellow might just as well be at school. I wonder what Adolphus Brown would think of being cooped up with a lot of children like this! It's his party to-night, and he's to have champagne and ices. I wish I were an only son."

"Thank you," said a chorus of voices from the floor. They were all sprawling about on the hearth-rug, pushing and struggling like so many kittens in a sack, and every now and then with a grumbled remonstrance:—

"Don't, Jack! you're treading on me."

"You needn't take all the fire, Tom."

"Keep your legs to yourself, Benjamin."

"It wasn't I," etc., with occasionally the feebler cry of a small sister,—

"Oh! you boys are so rough."

"And what are you girls, I wonder?" inquired the proprietor of the arm-chair, with cutting irony. "Whiney piney, whiney piney. I wish there were no such things as brothers and sisters!"

"You wish WHAT?" said a voice from the shadow by the door, as deep and impressive as that of the ghost in Hamlet.

The ten sprang up; but when the figure came into the firelight, they saw that it was no ghost, but Paterfamilias's old college friend, who spent most of his time abroad, and who, having no home or relatives of his own, had come to spend Christmas at his friend's vicarage. "You wish *what*?" he repeated.

"Well, brothers and sisters are a bore," was the reply. "One or two would be all very well; but just look, here are ten of us; and it just spoils everything. Whatever one does, the rest must do; whatever there is, the rest must share; whereas, if a fellow was an only son, he would have the whole—and by all the rules of arithmetic, one is better than a tenth."

"And by the same rules, ten is better than one," said the friend.

"Sold again!" sang out Master Jack from the floor, and went head over heels against the fender.

His brother boxed his ears with great promptitude; and went on— "Well, I don't care; confess, sir; isn't it rather a nuisance?"

Paterfamilias's friend looked very grave, and said quietly, "I don't think I am able to judge. I never had brother or sister but one, and he was drowned at sea. Whatever I have had, I have had the whole of, and would have given it away willingly for some one to give it to. I remember that I got a lot of sticks at last, and cut heads and faces to all of them, and carved names on their sides, and called them my brothers and sisters. If you want to know what I thought a nice number for a fellow to have, I can only say that I remember carving twenty-five. I used to stick them in the ground and talk to them. I have been only, and lonely, and alone, all my life, and have never felt the nuisance you speak of."

"I know what would be very nice," insinuated one of the sisters.

"What?"

"If you wouldn't mind telling us a very short story till supper-time."

"Well, what sort of a story is it to be?"

"Any sort," said Richard; "only not too true, if you please. I don't like stories like tracts. There was an usher at a school I was at, and he used to read tracts about good boys and bad boys to the fellows on Sunday afternoon. He always took out the real names, and put in the names of the fellows instead. Those who had done well in the week, he put in as good ones, and those who hadn't as the bad. He didn't like me, and I was always put in as a bad boy, and I came to so many untimely ends, I got sick of it. I was hanged twice, and transported once for sheep stealing; I committed suicide one week, and broke into the bank the next; I ruined three families, became a hopeless drunkard, and broke the hearts of my twelve distinct parents. I used to beg him to let me be reformed next week; but he said he never would till I did my Cæsar better. So, if you please, we'll have a story that can't be true."

"Very well," said the friend, laughing; "but if it isn't true, may I put you in? All the best writers, you know, draw their characters from their friends, nowadays. May I put you in?"

"Oh, certainly!" said Richard, placing himself in front of the fire, putting his feet on the hob, and stroking his curls with an air which seemed to imply that whatever he was put into would be highly favored.

The rest struggled, and pushed, and squeezed themselves into more modest but equally comfortable quarters; and after a few moments of thought, Paterfamilias's friend commenced the story of

MELCHIOR'S DREAM.

"Melchior is my hero. He was—well, he considered himself a young man, so we will consider him so too. He was not perfect; but in these days the taste in heroes is for a good deal of imperfection, not to say wickedness. He was not an only son. On the contrary, he had a great many brothers and sisters, and found them quite as objectionable as my friend Richard does."

"I smell a moral," murmured the said Richard.

"Your scent must be keen," said the story-teller, "for it is a long way off. Well, he had never felt them so objectionable as on one particular night, when the house being full of company, it was decided that the boys should sleep in 'barracks,' as they called it; that is, all in one large room."

"Thank goodness we have not come to that!" said the incorrigible Richard; but he was reduced to order by threats of being turned out, and contented himself with burning the soles of his boots against the bars of the grate in silence: and the friend continued:

"But this was not the worst. Not only was he, Melchior, to sleep in the same room with his brothers, but his bed being the longest and largest, his youngest brother was to sleep at the other end of it— foot to foot. True, by this means he got another pillow, for of course that little Hop-o'-my-thumb could do without one, and so he took his; but in spite of this, he determined that, sooner than submit to such an indignity, he would sit up all night. Accordingly, when all the rest were fast asleep, Melchior, with his boots off and his waistcoat easily unbuttoned, sat over the fire in the long lumber-room, which served that night as 'barracks'. He had refused to eat any supper down-stairs to mark his displeasure, and now repaid himself by a stolen meal according to his own taste. He had got a pork-pie, a little bread and cheese, some large onions to roast, a couple of raw apples, an orange, and papers of soda and tartaric acid to compound effervescing draughts. When these dainties were finished, he proceeded to warm some beer in a pan, with ginger, spice, and sugar, and then lay back in his chair and sipped it slowly, gazing before him, and thinking over his misfortunes.

"The night wore on, the fire got lower and lower; and still Melchior sat, with his eyes fixed on a dirty old print, that had hung above the mantel-piece for years, sipping his 'brew,' which was fast getting cold. The print represented an old man in a light costume, with a scythe in one hand, and an hour-glass in the other; and underneath the picture in flourishing capitals was the word TIME.

"'You're a nice old beggar,' said Melchior, dreamily. 'You look like an old haymaker, who has come to work in his shirt-sleeves, and forgotten the rest of his clothes. Time! time you went to the tailor's, I think.'

"This was very irreverent: but Melchior was not in a respectful mood; and as for the old man, he was as calm as any philosopher.

"The night wore on, and the fire got lower and lower, and at last went out altogether.

"'How stupid of me not to have mended it! said Melchior; but he had not mended it, and so there was nothing for it but to go to bed; and to bed he went accordingly.

"'But I won't go to sleep,' he said; 'no, no; I shall keep awake, and to-morrow they shall know that I have had a bad night.'

"So he lay in bed with his eyes wide open, and staring still at the old print, which he could see from his bed by the light of the candle, which he had left alight on the mantel-piece to keep him awake. The flame waved up and down, for the room was draughty; and, as the lights and shadows passed over the old man's face, Melchior almost fancied that it nodded to him, so he nodded back again; and as that tired him he shut his eyes for a few seconds. When he opened them again there was no longer any doubt—the old man's head was moving; and not only his head, but his legs, and his whole body. Finally, he put his feet out of the frame, and prepared to step right over the mantel-piece, candle, and all.

"'Take care,' Melchior tried to say, 'you'll set fire to your shirt.' But he could not utter a sound; and the old man arrived safely on the floor, where he seemed to grow larger and larger, till he was fully the size of a man, but still with the same scythe and hour-glass, and the same airy costume. Then he came across the room, and sat down by Melchior's bedside.

"'Who are you?' said Melchior, feeling rather creepy.

"'Time,' said his visitor, in a deep voice, which sounded as if it came from a distance.

"'Oh, to be sure, yes! In copper plate capitals.'

"'What's in copper-plate capitals?' inquired Time.

"'Your name, under the print.'

"'Very likely,' said Time.

"Melchior felt more and more uneasy. 'You must be very cold,' he said. 'Perhaps you would feel warmer if you went back into the picture.'

"'Not at all.' said Time; 'I have come on purpose to see you.'

"'I have not the pleasure of knowing you,' said Melchior, trying to keep his teeth from chattering.

"'There are not many people who have a personal acquaintance with me,' said his visitor. 'You have an advantage,—I am your godfather.'

"'Indeed,' said Melchior; 'I never heard of it.'

"'Yes,' said his visitor; 'and you will find it a great advantage.'

"'Would you like to put on my coat?' said Melchior, trying to be civil.

"'No, thank you,' was the answer. 'You will want it yourself. We must be driving soon.'

"'Driving!' said Melchior.

"'Yes,' was the answer: 'all the world is driving; and you must drive; and here come your brothers and sisters.'

"Melchior sat up; and there they were, sure enough, all dressed, and climbing one after the other on to the bed—*his* bed!

"There was that little minx of a sister with her curls. There was that clever brother, with his untidy hair and bent shoulders, who was just as bad the other way, and was forever moping and reading. There was that little Hop-o'-my-thumb, as lively as any of them, a young monkey, the worst of all; who was always in mischief, and consorting with the low boys in the village. There was the second brother, who was Melchior's chief companion, and against whom he had no particular quarrel. And there was the little pale lame sister, whom he dearly loved; but whom, odd to say, he never tried to improve at all. There were others who were all tiresome in their respective ways; and one after the other they climbed up.

"'What are you doing, getting on to my bed?' inquired the indignant brother, as soon as he could speak.

"'Don't you know the difference between a bed and a coach, godson?' said Time, sharply.

"Melchior was about to retort, but, on looking round, he saw that they were really in a large sort of coach with very wide windows. 'I thought I was in bed,' he muttered. 'What can I have been dreaming of?'

"'What, indeed!' said the godfather. 'But be quick, and sit close, for you have all to get in; you are all brothers and sisters.'

"'Must families be together?' inquired Melchior, dolefully.

"'Yes, at first,' was the answer; 'they get separated in time. In fact, every one has to cease driving sooner or later. I drop them on the road at different stages, according to my orders,' and he showed a bundle of papers in his hands; 'but as I favor you, I will tell you in confidence that I have to drop all your brothers and sisters before you. There, you four oldest sit on this side, you five others there, and the little one must stand or be nursed.'

"'Ugh!' said Melchior, 'the coach would be well enough if one was alone; but what a squeeze with all these brats! I say, go pretty quick, will you?'

"'I will,' said Time, 'if you wish it. But beware that you cannot change your mind. If I go quicker for your sake, I shall never go slow again; if slower, I shall not again go quick; and I only favor you so far, because you are my godson. Here, take the check-string; when you want me, pull it, and speak through the tube. Now we're off.'

"Whereupon the old man mounted the box, and took the reins. He had no whip; but when he wanted to start, he shook the hour-glass, and off they went. Then Melchior saw that the road where they were driving was very broad, and so filled with vehicles of all kinds that he could not see the hedges. The noise and crowd and dust were very great; and to Melchior all seemed delightfully exciting. There was every sort of conveyance, from the grandest coach to the humblest donkey-cart; and they seemed to have enough to do to escape being run over. Among all the gay people there were many whom he knew; and a very nice thing it seemed to be to drive among all the grandees, and to show his handsome face at the window, and bow and smile to his acquaintance. Then it appeared to be the fashion to wrap one's self in a tiger-skin rug, and to look at life through an opera-glass, and old Time had kindly put one of each into the coach.

"But here again Melchior was much troubled by his brothers and sisters. Just at the moment when he was wishing to look most fashionable and elegant, one or other of them would pull away the rug, or drop the glass, or quarrel, or romp, or do something that spoiled the effect. In fact, one and all, they 'just spoilt everything;' and the more he scolded, the worse they became. The 'minx' shook her curls, and flirted through the window with a handsome but ill-tempered looking man on a fine horse, who praised her 'golden locks,' as he called them; and oddly enough, when Melchior said that the man was a lout, and that the locks in question were corkscrewy carrot shavings, she only seemed to like the man and his compliments the more. Meanwhile, the untidy brother pored over his book, or if he came to the window, it was only to ridicule the fine ladies and gentlemen, so Melchior sent him to Coventry. Then Hop-o'-my-thumb had taken to make signs and exchange jokes with some disreputable-looking youths in a dog-cart; and when his brother would have put him to 'sit still like a gentleman' at the bottom of the coach, he seemed positively to prefer his low companions; and the rest were little better.

"Poor Melchior! Surely there never was a clearer case of a young gentleman's comfort destroyed solely by other people's perverse determination to be happy in their own way instead of in his.

"At last he lost patience, and pulling the check-string, bade Godfather Time drive as fast as he could.

"Godfather Time frowned, but shook his glass all the same, and away they went at a famous pace. All at once they came to a stop.

"'Now for it,' said Melchior; 'here goes one at any rate.'

"Time called out the name of the second brother over his shoulder; and the boy stood up, and bade his brothers and sisters good-bye.

"'It is time that I began to push my way in the world,' said he, and passed out of the coach and in among the crowd.

"'You have taken the only quiet boy,' said Melchior to the godfather, angrily. 'Drive fast, now, for pity's sake; and let us get rid of the tiresome ones.'

"And fast enough they drove, and dropped first one and then the other; but the sisters, and the reading boy, and the youngest still remained.

"'What are you looking at?' said Melchior to the lame sister.

"'At a strange figure in the crowd,' she answered.

"'I see nothing,' said Melchior. But on looking again after a while, he did see a figure wrapped in a cloak, gliding in and out among the people, unnoticed, if not unseen.

"'Who is it?' Melchior asked of the godfather.

"'A friend of mine,' Time answered. 'His name is Death.'

"Melchior shuddered, more especially as the figure had now come up to the coach, and put its hand in through the window, on which, to his horror, the lame sister laid hers and smiled. At this moment the coach stopped.

"'What are you doing?' shrieked Melchior. 'Drive on! drive on!'

"But even while he sprang up to seize the check-string the door had opened, the pale sister's face had dropped upon the shoulder of the figure in the cloak, and he had carried her away; and Melchior stormed and raved in vain.

"'To take her, and to leave the rest! Cruel! cruel!'

"In his rage and grief, he hardly knew it when the untidy brother was called, and putting his book under his arm, slipped out of the coach without looking to the right or left. Presently the coach stopped again; and when Melchior looked up the door was open, and at it was the fine man on the fine horse, who was lifting the sister on to the saddle before him. 'What fool's game are you playing?' said Melchior, angrily. 'I know that man. He is both ill-tempered and a bad character.'

"'You never told her so before,' muttered young Hop-o'-my-thumb.

"'Hold your tongue,' said Melchior. 'I forbade her to talk to him, which was enough.'

"'I don't want to leave you; but he cares for me, and you don't,' sobbed the sister; and she was carried away.

"When she had gone, the youngest brother slid down from his corner and came up to Melchior.

"'We are alone now, brother,' he said; 'let us be good friends. May I sit on the front seat with you, and have half the rug? I will be very good and polite, and will have nothing more to do with those fellows, if you will talk to me.'

"Now Melchior really rather liked the idea; but as his brother seemed to be in a submissive mood, he thought he would take the opportunity of giving him a good lecture, and would then graciously relent and forgive. So he began by asking him if he thought that he was fit company for him (Melchior), what he thought that gentlefolks would say to a boy who had been playing with such youths as young Hop-o'-my-thumb had, and whether the said youths were not scoundrels? And when the boy refused to say that they were, (for they had been kind to him,) Melchior said that his tastes were evidently as bad as ever, and even hinted at the old transportation threat. This was too much; the boy went angrily back to his window corner, and Melchior—like too many of us!—lost the opportunity of making peace for the sake of wagging his own tongue.

"'But he will come round in a few minutes,' he thought. A few minutes passed, however, and there was no sign. A few minutes more, and there was a noise, a shout; Melchior looked up, and saw that the boy had jumped through the open window into the road, and had been picked up by the men in the dog-cart, and was gone.

"And so at last my hero was alone. At first he enjoyed it very much. But though every one allowed him to be the finest young fellow on the road, yet nobody seemed to care for the fact as much as he did; they talked, and complimented, and stared at him, but he got tired of it. Sometimes he saw the youngest brother, looking each time more wild and reckless; and sometimes the sister, looking more and more miserable; but he saw no one else.

"At last there was a stir among the people, and all heads were turned towards the distance, as if looking for something. Melchior asked what it was, and was told that the people were looking for a man, the hero of many battles, who had won honor for himself and for his country in foreign lands, and who was coming home. Everybody stood up and gazed, Melchior with them. Then the crowd parted, and the hero came on. No one asked whether he were handsome or genteel, whether he kept good company, or wore a tiger-skin rug, or looked through an opera-glass? They knew what he had *done*, and it was enough.

"He was a bronzed, hairy man, with one sleeve empty, and a breast covered with stars; but in his face, brown with sun and wind, overgrown with hair, and scarred with wounds, Melchior saw his second brother! There was no doubt of it. And the brother himself, though he bowed kindly in answer to the greetings showered on him, was gazing anxiously for the old coach, where he used to ride and be so uncomfortable, in that time to which he now looked back as the happiest of his life.

"'I thank you, gentlemen. I am indebted to you, gentlemen. I have been away long. I am going home.'

"'Of course he is!' shouted Melchior, waving his arms widely with pride and joy. 'He is coming home; to this coach, where he was—oh, it seems but an hour ago; Time goes so fast. We were great friends when we were young together. My brother and I, ladies and gentlemen, the hero and I—my brother—the hero with the stars upon his breast—he is coming home!'

"Alas! what avail stars and ribbons on a breast where the life-blood is trickling slowly from a little wound? The crowd looked anxious; the hero came on, but more slowly, with his dim eyes straining for the old coach; and Melchior stood with his arms held out in silent agony. But just when he was beginning to hope, and the brothers seemed about to meet, a figure passed between—a figure in a cloak.

"'I have seen you many times, friend, face to face,' said the hero; 'but now I would fain have waited for a little while.'

"'To enjoy his well-earned honors,' murmured the crowd.

"'Nay,' he said, 'not that; but to see my home, and my brothers and sisters. But if it may not be, friend Death, I am ready, and tired, too.' With that he held out his hand, and Death lifted up the hero of many battles like a child, and carried him away, stars, and ribbons, and all.

"'Cruel Death!' cried Melchior; 'was there no one else in all this crowd, that you must take him?'

"His friends condoled with him; but they soon went on their own ways; and the hero seemed to be forgotten; and Melchior, who had lost all pleasure in the old bowings and chattings, sat idly gazing out of the window, to see if he could see any one for whom he cared. At last, in a grave dark man, who was sitting on a horse, and making a speech to the crowd, he recognized his clever untidy brother.

"'What is that man talking about?' he asked of some one near him.

"'That man!' was the answer. 'Don't you know? He is *the* man of the time. He is a philosopher. Everybody goes to hear him. He has found out that—well—that everything is a mistake.'

"'Has he corrected it?' said Melchior.

"'You had better hear for yourself,' said the man. 'Listen.'

"Melchior listened, and a cold, clear voice rang upon his ear, saying,—

"'The world of fools will go on as they have ever done; but to the wise few, to whom I address myself, I would say, Shake off at once and forever the fancies and feelings, the creeds and customs that shackle you, and be true. We have come to a time when wise men will not be led blindfold in the footsteps of their predecessors, but will tear away the bandage, and see for themselves. I have torn away mine, and looked. There is no Faith—it is shaken to its rotten foundation; there is no Hope—it is disappointed every day; there is no Love at all. There is nothing for any man or for each, but his fate; and he is happiest and wisest who can meet it most unmoved.'

"'It is a lie!' shouted Melchior. 'I feel it to be so in my heart. A wicked, foolish lie! Oh! was it to teach such evil folly as this that you left home and us, my brother? Oh, come back! come back!'

"The philosopher turned his head coldly, and smiled. 'I thank the gentleman who spoke,' he said, still in the same cold voice, 'for his bad opinion, and for his good wishes. I think the gentleman spoke of home and kindred. My experience of life has led me to find that home is most valued when it is left, and kindred most dear when they are parted. I have happily freed myself from such inconsistencies. I am glad to know that fate can tear me from no place that I care for more than the next where it shall deposit me, nor take away any friends that I value more than those it leaves. I recommend a similar self-emancipation to the gentleman who did me the honor of speaking.'

"With this the philosopher went his way, and the crowd followed him.

"'There is a separation more bitter than death,' said Melchior.

"At last he pulled the check-string, and called to Godfather Time in an humble, entreating voice.

"'It is not your fault,' he began; 'it is not your fault, godfather; but this drive has been altogether wrong. Let us turn back and begin again. Let us all get in afresh and begin again.'

"But what a squeeze with all the brats!' said Godfather Time, ironically.

"'We should be so happy,' murmured Melchior, humbly; 'and it is very cold and chilly; we should keep each other warm.'

"'You have the tiger-skin rug and the opera-glass, you know,' said Time.

"Ah, do not speak of me!" cried Melchior, earnestly. 'I am thinking of them. There is plenty of room; the little one can sit on my knee; and we shall be so happy. The truth is, godfather, that I have been wrong. I have gone the wrong way to work. A little more love, and kindness, and forbearance might have kept my sisters with us, might have led the little one to better tastes and pleasures, and have taught the other by experience the truth of the faith and hope and love which he now reviles. Oh, I have sinned! I have sinned! Let us turn back, Godfather Time, and begin again. And oh! drive very slowly, for partings come only too soon.'

"'I am sorry,' said the old man in the same bitter tone as before, 'to disappoint your rather unreasonable wishes. What you say is admirably true, with this misfortune, that your good intentions are too late. Like the rest of the world, you are ready to seize the opportunity when it is past. You should have been kind *then*. You should have advised *then*. You should have yielded *then*. You should have loved your brothers and sisters while you had them. It is too late now.'

"With this he drove on, and spoke no more, and poor Melchior stared sadly out of the window. As he was gazing at the crowd, he suddenly saw the dog-cart, in which were his brother and his wretched companions. Oh, how old and worn he looked! and how ragged his clothes were! The men seemed to be trying to persuade him to do something that he did not like, and they began to quarrel; but in the midst of the dispute he turned his head, and caught sight of the old coach; and Melchior, seeing this, waved his hands, and beckoned with all his might. The brother seemed doubtful; but Melchior waved harder, and (was it fancy?) Time seemed to go slower. The brother made up his mind; he turned and jumped from the dog-cart as he had jumped from the old coach long ago, and, ducking in and out among the horses and carriages, ran for his life. The men came after him; but he ran like the wind—pant, pant, nearer, nearer; at last the coach was reached, and Melchior seized the prodigal by his rags and dragged him in.

"Oh, thank God, I have got you safe, my brother!'

'But what a brother! with wasted body and sunken eyes; with the old curly hair turned to matted locks, that clung faster to his face than the rags did to his trembling limbs; what a sight for the opera-glasses of the crowd! Yet poor Hop-o'-my-thumb was on the front seat at last, with Melchior kneeling at his feet, and fondly stroking the head that rested against him.

"Has powder come into fashion, brother?' he said. 'Your hair is streaked with white.'

"If it has,' said the other, laughing, 'your barber is better than mine, Melchior, for your head is as white as snow.'

"Is it possible? are we so old? has Time gone so very fast? But what are you staring at through the window? I shall be jealous of that crowd, brother.'

"I am not looking at the crowd,' said the prodigal in a low voice; 'but I see——'

"You see what?' said Melchior.

"A figure in a cloak, gliding in and out——'

"Melchior sprang up in horror. 'No! no!' he cried, hoarsely. 'No! surely no!'

"Surely yes! Too surely the well-known figure came on; and the prodigal's sunken eyes looked more sunken still as he gazed. As for Melchior, he neither spoke nor moved, but stood in a silent agony, terrible to see. All at once a thought seemed to strike him; he seized his brother, and pushed him to the farthest corner of the seat, and then planted himself firmly at the door, just as Death came up and put his hand into the coach. Then he spoke in a low, steady voice, more piteous than cries or tears.

"'I humbly beseech you, good Death, if you must take one of us, to take me. I have had a long drive, and many comforts and blessings, and am willing, if unworthy, to go. He has suffered much, and had no pleasure; leave him for a little to enjoy the drive in peace, just for a very little; he has suffered so much, and I have been so much to blame; let me go instead of him.'

"Poor Melchior! In vain he laid both his hands in Death's outstretched palm; they fell to him again as if they had passed through air; he was pushed aside—Death passed into the coach—'one was taken and the other left.'

"As the cloaked figure glided in and out among the crowd, many turned to look at his sad burden, though few heeded him. Much was said; but the general voice of the crowd was this: 'Ah! he is gone, is he? Well! a born rascal! It must be a great relief to his brother!' A conclusion which was about as wise, and about as near the truth, as the world's conclusions generally are. As for

Melchior, he neither saw the figure nor heard the crowd, for he had fallen senseless among the cushions.

"When he came to his senses, he found himself lying still upon his face; and so bitter was his loneliness and grief, that he lay still and did not move. He was astonished, however, by the (as it seemed to him) unusual silence. The noise of the carriage had been deafening, and now there was not a sound. Was he deaf? or had the crowd gone? He opened his eyes. Was he blind? or had the night come? He sat right up, and shook himself, and looked again. The crowd was gone; so, for matter of that, was the coach; and so was Godfather Time. He had not been lying among cushions, but among pillows; he was not in any vehicle of any kind, but in bed. The room was dark, and very still; but through the 'barracks' window, which had no blind, he saw the winter sun pushing through the mist, like a red-hot cannon-ball hanging in the frosty trees; and in the yard outside, the cocks were crowing.

"There was no longer any doubt that he was safe in his old home; but where were his brothers and sisters? With a beating heart he crept to the other end of the bed; and there lay the prodigal, with no haggard cheeks or sunken eyes, no gray locks or miserable rags, but a rosy, yellow-haired urchin fast asleep, with his head upon his arm. 'I took his pillow,' muttered Melchior, self-reproachfully.

"A few minutes later, young Hop-o'-my-thumb, (whom Melchior dared not lose sight of for fear he should melt away,) seated comfortably on his brother's back, and wrapped up in a blanket, was making a tour of the 'barracks.'

"'It's an awful lark,' said he, shivering with a mixture of cold and delight.

"If not exactly a *lark*, it was a very happy tour to Melchior, as, hope gradually changing into certainty, he recognized his brothers in one shapeless lump after the other in the little beds. There they all were, sleeping peacefully in a happy home, from the embryo hero to the embryo philosopher, who lay with the invariable book upon his pillow, and his hair looking (as it always did) as if he lived in a high wind.

"'I say,' whispered Melchior, pointing to him, 'what did he say the other day about being a parson?'

"'He said he should like to be one,' returned Hop-o'-my-thumb; 'but you said he would frighten away the congregation with his looks.'

"'He will make a capital parson,' said Melchior, hastily, 'and I shall tell him so to-morrow. And when I'm the squire here, he shall be vicar, and I'll subscribe to all his dodges without a grumble. I'm the eldest son. And I say, don't you think we could brush his hair for him in a morning, till he learns to do it himself?'

"'Oh, I will!' was the lively answer; 'I'm an awful dab at brushing. Look how I brush your best hat!'

"'True,' said Melchior. 'Where are the girls to-night?'

"'In the little room at the end of the long passage,' said Hop o'-my-thumb, trembling with increased chilliness and enjoyment. 'But you're never going there! we shall wake the company, and they will all come out to see what's the matter.'

"'I shouldn't care if they did,' said Melchior, 'it would make it feel more real.'

"As he did not understand this sentiment, Hop-o'-my-thumb said nothing, but held on very tightly; and they crept softly down the cold gray passage in the dawn. The girls' door was open; for the girls were afraid of robbers, and left their bed-room door wide open at night, as a natural and obvious means of self-defence. The girls slept together; and the frill of the pale sister's prim little night-cap was buried in the other one's uncovered curls.

"'How you do tremble!' whispered Hop-o'-my-thumb; 'are you cold?' This inquiry received no answer; and after some minutes he spoke again. 'I say, how very pretty they look! don't they?'

"But for some reason or other, Melchior seemed to have lost his voice; but he stooped down and kissed both the girls very gently, and then the two brothers crept back along the passage to the 'barracks.'

"'One thing more,' said Melchior; and they went up to the mantel-piece. 'I will lend you my bow and arrow to-morrow, on one condition——'

"'Anything!' was the reply, in an enthusiastic whisper.

"'That you take that old picture for a target, and never let me see it again.'

"It was very ungrateful! but perfection is not in man; and there was something in Melchior's muttered excuse,—

"'I couldn't stand another night of it.'

"Hop-o'-my-thumb was speedily put to bed again, to get warm, this time with both the pillows; but Melchior was too restless to sleep, so he resolved to have a shower-bath and to dress. After which he knelt down by the window, and covered his face with his hands.

"'He's saying very long prayers,' thought Hop-o'-my-thumb, glancing at him from his warm nest; 'and what a jolly humor he is in this morning!'

"Still, the young head was bent and the handsome face hidden; and Melchior was finding his life every moment more real and more happy. For there was hardly a thing, from the well-filled 'barracks' to the brother bedfellow, that had been a hardship last night, which this morning did not seem a blessing. He rose at last, and stood in the sunshine, which was now pouring in; a smile was on his lips, and on his face were two drops, which, if they were water, had not come from the shower-bath, or from any bath at all."

"Is that the end?" inquired the young lady on his knee, as the story-teller paused here.

"Yes, that is the end."

"It's a beautiful story," she murmured, thoughtfully; "but what an extraordinary one! I don't think I could have dreamt such a wonderful dream."

"Do you think you could have eaten such a wonderful supper?" said the friend, twisting his moustaches.

After this point, the evening's amusements were thoroughly successful. Richard took his smoking boots from the fireplace, and was called upon for various entertainments for which he was famous.

The door opened at last, and Paterfamilias entered with Materfamilias (whose headache was better), and followed by the candles. A fresh log was then thrown upon the fire, the yule cakes and furmety were put upon the table, and everybody drew round to supper; and Paterfamilias announced that, although he could not give the materials to play with, he had no objection now to a bowl of moderate punch for all, and that Richard might compound it. This was delightful; and as he sat by his father ladling away to the rest, Adolphus Brown could hardly have felt more jovial, even with the champagne and ices.

The rest sat with radiant faces and shining heads in goodly order; and at the bottom of the table, by Materfamilias, was the friend, as happy in his unselfish sympathy as if his twenty-five sticks had come to life, and were supping with him. As happy—nearly— as if a certain woman's grave had never been dug under the southern sun that could not save her, and as if the children gathered round him were those of whose faces he had often dreamt, but might never see.

His health had been drunk, and everybody else's too, when, just as supper was coming to a close, Richard (who had been sitting in thoughtful silence for some minutes) got up with sudden resolution, and said,—

"I want to propose Mr. What's-his-name's health on my own account. I want to thank him for his story, which had only one mistake in it. Melchior should have kept the effervescing papers to put into the beer; it's a splendid drink! Otherwise it was first-rate; though it hit me rather hard. I want to say that though I didn't mean all I said about being an only son, (when a fellow gets put out he doesn't know what he means,) yet I know I was quite wrong, and the story is quite right. I want particularly to say that I'm very glad there are so many of us, for the more, you know, the merrier. I wouldn't change father or mother, brothers or sisters, with any one in the world. It couldn't be better, we couldn't be happier. We are all together, and to-morrow is Christmas-Day. Thank God."

Read by the Landlord.

> "A jolly negation, who took upon

> him the ordering of the bills of

> fare."

> Lamb.

MR. GRAPEWINE'S CHRISTMAS DINNER.

"My dear," said Mr. Grapewine, over the dinner-table, about a fortnight before Christmas,—"how many days to Christmas?"

Mrs. Grapewine counted on her fingers; looked a little uncertain up towards the ceiling, and at last applied to the calendar on the wall behind her, exclaiming, when she had mentally calculated the time,—

"Week and six days; comes on Thursday."

"True," said Mr. Grapewine, and he fell to devouring the residuum of his meal, a very savory mixture, which he swallowed with an amazing relish.

"There!" said he, after the last sip of coffee, "I believe I don't want another thing to eat till Christmas-day. Mrs. G., you have the art of concocting the most appetizing meals. I never seem to get enough of them."

"Two a day!" suggested Mrs. Grapewine, in her sharp manner.

"No, no, no! Mrs. G., you *are* an experienced cateress, that I confess. But there is a delicacy in the thing which two such meals a day would utterly destroy. You misunderstand me? It is the expectancy, the snuffing up of the fumes beforehand, the very consciousness of your inability to cope with it, which makes such a meal delicious. Now two a day would leave a man no chance to get properly hungry. That's the point. It is the preparation, the deferred hope, which render a good dinner one of the completest luxuries of life. The hungrier one is, the more prolonged the satisfaction of the palate. I don't think I have ever been hungry to the fullest extent of my capacity in my life."

"Trip across Sahara!" interpolated Mrs. Grapewine.

"Yes, that would do, my dear; but I think we could accomplish it at home by artificial means. I *think* we could. Fasting would not do, because the appetite would at last grow unable to discriminate. Drugs would enfeeble it. (I'll thank you for another cup of coffee, my dear. Ah, delicious cup of coffee!)—Drugs would enfeeble it. There is really no direct stimulant that I know of; but I *think* we could intensify the appetite by a little course of diplomacy. Let us eat frugally—sandwiches, crackers and cheese, potted meats—for the next two weeks; and, if you please, cook us at each luncheon-time, as a sort of stimulating accompaniment, some odorous dish,—roast-beef, stuffed leg of lamb, roast turkey, codfish, anything with an odor,—which we shall smell, but not taste of. Don't you see, madam?"

"No!"

"Don't you see that our stomachs will yearn for these strong delicacies, and, going unsatisfied, will relish them the more when we at last attack them?"

"No!"

"You have something to propose then, my dear. What is it? What have you to propose?"

"Turkish bath!"

"What a woman you are. A Turkish bath! How, Mrs. Grapewine, can a Turkish bath tickle a man's appetite? How can a Turkish——"

"Empty stomach."

"Ah, now I begin to see: a Turkish bath on an empty stomach. Yes, yes; very good. But, perhaps, if we tried my plan and yours together, we should arrive at the ideal appetite. I think a Christmas feast composed of guests each with such an appetite would be nearly the greatest pleasure we can know. Well, well, madam, let us think of it (The bell? Yes, quite through)," and, saying this last to the tinkling of the little silver bell, Mr. Grapewine got up from the table, undid the napkin from his neck, and yawned both his arms quite over his fat, rosy head as he trode towards the door. Mrs. Grapewine's step was like her conversation,—sharp and decisive. She took her husband's arm in an angular manner and led him, still yawning, to the sofa in the library, where she set herself over against him, ready to hear his plans.

"Let us have a Christmas banquet, my dear," Mr. Grapewine steadily rubbed his eyes and yawned.

"Who?" said Mrs. Grapewine.

"Why, Totty and his wife, and Colonel Killiam, and—and Dr. Tuggle and lady, and old Mrs. Gildenfenny and—and——" Mr. Grapewine snored.

"Who?" said Mrs. Grapewine, somewhat loudly.

—"And—and—Pill."

"Who's Pill?" said she.

"Why—oh, I mean your poor cousin Pillet. It would be a kindness to him, you know."

"Yes," said she.

"Will that be enough? Let me see, that is seven—nine with us two."

"Quite enough," said she. And so Mr. Grapewine, arousing himself, rose from the sofa, put on his hat and coat, and went out to his business.

He was full of the idea. He talked about it to his clerks at the store. He looked into restaurant windows, humming a tune in the excess of his delight. He looked into bakers' windows and confectionery shops, and a whiff of frying bacon from a little blind court he passed almost set him dancing. Indeed, Mr. Grapewine was a man of juvenile impulse. In figure as well as character he seemed rather to have expanded into a larger sort of babyhood than to have left that stage of his life behind. His face was broad and rosy and whiskerless, his hands were round and well-dimpled, and his body chubby to a degree. Once an idea got possession of him, he was its bondsman until another conquered it and enslaved him anew. But, really loving good cheer above everything else, his latest whim tickled him into laughter whenever it entered his mind. It was the happiest idea of his life.

"Why, sir," he said to his book-keeper, "I think if a man would practise my system he could easily eat a whole turkey—not to speak of other dishes—at a meal. Magnificent idea! William. I wonder no one ever thought of it before. Wonderful!"

"A little bilious, sir," said William.

"Bilious! bilious! Why, my man, how can anything produce biliousness in an empty stomach? No; it may bring inertia,—the Lotos does that,—but never biliousness."

In the evening, Mr. Grapewine visited the Turkish baths and learned all about them before he went home. He encountered another idea on his way thither, and was taken captive by it without resistance. He could not—it would never do—it would not be courteous to eat so plentifully in the presence of guests whose appetites were merely natural. Nor could he well ask them to take the stimulating course he proposed for himself. But they *could* take a Turkish bath, and it would be quite a neat little social device to enclose a ticket for a bath with each invitation.

"There, madam!" he said to Mrs. Grapewine, "I think that's perfect. We shall have the heartiest, merriest dinner on Christmas-day that man ever devoured. Bring pen and paper, and I'll write to all the guests immediately, ma'am."

After a moment's scratching of the pen, Mr. Grapewine leaned back in his chair and held off the wet sheet at arm's length, reading with strong emphasis as follows,—

"Dear Captain Killiam,—Mrs. Grapewine and myself would be most happy to have you join a small company of friends at our house on Christmas-day, for dinner, at one p.m. The affair will be quite informal, and, to add to the thorough enjoyment of it, I enclose a coupon for a Turkish-bath, which please use on Christmas morning before the hour named.

"Yours, sincerely,

"George Grapewine."

By the next morning Mr. Grapewine's invitations had found their way to the breakfast-tables of all his expected guests.

Mr. Pillet's breakfast-table was composed of the top of a flat trunk, and to find its way there the invitation went up three pairs of stairs. Mr. Pillet was a writer, and his income was by no means as great as his ability. He had often to point out a similar disparity in the lives of other writers, because this was his one way of accounting for his want of success. He did not write books, to be sure. He only wrote poetical advertisements. But they were printed and paid for, and this gave him a sort of prestige among his less lucky friends. He was seedy; only moderately clean, and wholly unshaven, thus avoiding, by one happy invention, both soap and the barber. Fierce he was to look at, with his rugged beard and eyebrows, and fierce in his resentment of the world's indifference. A Christmas invitation to the Grapewine's made his eyes glisten with delight: a good dinner, guests to tell his tale to, and women, lovely women, who would sympathize with his unrequited hopes. He read on:

"I enclose a ticket for a Turkish bath——"

"Great heavens!" he cried, "what can this mean?"

He read the words again, and then read the coupon.

"Insulted! Insulted by a man I have ever befriended. He must apologize. I'll shake the words from his throat. I'll—I'll not eat another mouthful till I have his apology! Turkish bath! Why——" and Mr. Pillet walked violently—gesticulating, with the open note in his hand—up and down the creaking floor of his apartment. He did not finish his breakfast, but put on his hat—perhaps forgetting an overcoat—and hurried down-stairs.

Colonel Killiam took breakfast at the "Furlough Club." He perused Mr. Grapewine's note with a majestic condescension, and decided to go to the dinner, where, of course, those present would recognize his superior rank. Each sentence he read was sandwiched between two sips of chocolate, and he reached the latter clause only by slow degrees. When he got that far, the colonel started to his feet and sternly summoned the waiter.

"Ask Major Fobbs to call at my table as soon as he can."

The waiter obeyed, and Major Fobbs followed him back to the colonel's table.

"Major," said the colonel, "will you please spell those words?"

"T-u-r-k-i-s-h b-a-t-h, Turkish bath," read the major.

"Thank heaven, I am still rational!" said the colonel. "I feared reason was dethroned. Thank you, major. Good-day," and Colonel Killiam strode out of the room, rigid with indignation.

Old Mrs. Gildenfenny received her invitation over a breakfast-table that stood against her bedside. The note was handed in by an aged servant, who thereupon leaned over her mistress's shoulder and helped her to read it. Mrs. Gildenfenny was an energetic old lady; but she loved, most of all things in the world, her idle hour in bed of a morning with a smoking meal of hot-cakes and coffee at her elbow. She disliked, most of all things in the world, to be robbed of this comfort, and she hated the being who committed such an offence with a vehemence which was her chief characteristic. The two old women read Mrs. Gildenfenny's note aloud en duet, with now and then a pleased comment. Mrs. Gildenfenny said she would wear her green silk, and gave directions, as she read on, about her shoes, her hair, her linen and twenty articles of her toilet that came into her mind at mention of dining out.

"Lord a-mercy!" says Mrs. Gildenfenny, when she had read a little further; "Lord a-mercy! if I'm not decent, why does he ask me? Why don't he say, at once, 'Please wash yourself before you come; and if you can't afford soap and water, here's a ticket'? Susan, get me up! Dress me right away! I must have this explained."

"But your breakfast, ma'am," says Susan.

"Eat? eat? with such a thing on my mind? No! I'll go at once to his house!" and in a few moments Mrs. Gildenfenny also went out.

Mr. and Mrs. Totty were served with their invitation over a breakfast-table where meekness and humility were administered with the rolls and poured out with the weak cambric tea of the little ones. The meal was an impressive ceremony, where discourses on duty and against excess of the palate were often the only relishes present.

Mr. Totty would paint the miseries of the epicure, and Mrs. Totty those of the dyspeptic, in words of eloquence which made milk-and-sugar-and-water a liquid of priceless moral value, though they never succeeded in strengthening its nutritive effects. While the eldest Totty had answered the postman's summons, Mr. Totty was exhorting his youngest son to avoid butter to his bread as a pitfall through which he must eventually come to a state of depravity too dreadful to be put in words. He opened the envelope very deliberately, supposing it to contain a bill, but with a smile on his benevolent face which betokened a reverent spirit under suffering. As he read the opening lines and went onward, the smile passed through the stages of surprise, gratification, appetite, eagerness, and then passed into a look of doubt. He laughed in a gently acid way, and said,—

"My dear, Mr. Grapewine invites us to a Christmas dinner, which, of course, we could not attend——"

"Why not?" exclaims Mrs. Totty, eagerly.

"Which it would do gross injury to our principles to attend," continued Mr. Totty; "and I will call on him, with our refusal, this morning, myself."

Mrs. Totty resignedly helped him on with his overcoat, and submitted to the mildly spoken decree which was law in the house of the Tottys.

In a short time her husband went out with the invitation in his pocket and a look of unusual benevolence in his eyes.

Dr. Tuggle and lady read the invitation together over their breakfast-table, and fell to quarrelling so dreadfully about the purport of Mr. Grapewine's singular request, that the doctor rushed from the house, threatening to pull Mr. Grapewine's nose, and to divorce himself forever from his hateful spouse.

On this same morning Mr. Grapewine's bell was rung five times, at very short intervals, in the most tremendously violent manner, and five loud altercations took place in the hall between the servant and the five callers.

"Where is he?"

"Bring him down, or I'll go up after him!"

"What does he mean by it?"

"Insult a respectable lady!"

"Let me catch him, that's all!"

"Where has he gone?"

"I'll send him a challenge by Fobbs!"

"Where's his wife?"

This was what Mr. Grapewine, listening at the top of the stairs, heard in a confused tumult in his parlor. He could not understand it. He was extremely agitated; but the servant insisted on his going down, and he did so, clad in a loose morning dress and slippers. As he entered the parlor-door he was met by four furious gentlemen and an elderly lady, flourishing his invitations in their hands and crying hotly for explanations.

"What do you mean, sir? What do you mean by alluding to my—my toilet in this impertinent manner?" said Colonel Killiam.

The light began to flow in upon Mr. Grapewine's puzzled understanding. He confessed his mistake, and would have urged them to forget it and come to the dinner as if nothing had happened, but before he could do so he found himself alone in the room, with five notes of invitation on the floor at his feet, and nothing but the remembrance of one of the best ideas he had ever had in his life.

end of book ii.

The End